MW00710687

SECURITY

IN THE

BOARDROOM:

THE IMPACT OF PHYSICAL & NETWORK SECURITY ON CORPORATIONS AND WHAT EXECUTIVES NEED TO KNOW AND DO ABOUT IT.

By Mark S.A. Smith

Also By Mark S.A. Smith

Guerrilla Trade Show Selling
Guerrilla TeleSelling
Guerrilla Negotiating
Linux in the Boardroom
VoIP in the Boardroom

SECURITY

IN THE

BOARDROOM:

THE IMPACT OF PHYSICAL & NETWORK SECURITY ON CORPORATIONS AND WHAT EXECUTIVES NEED TO KNOW AND DO ABOUT IT.

Library of Congress Control Number: 2005900983

Published by
Outsource Channel Executives, Inc.
12 North 33rd Street
Colorado Springs, CO 80904
United States of America
www.OCEinc.com

ISBN 0-9749289-7-6 Hardcover
ISBN 0-9749289-8-4 Soft cover
First Printing
v1.0

Printed in the United States of America.

Disclaimer

Neither the author nor the publisher assumes any responsibility for errors, inaccuracies, or omissions. Any slights of people or organizations are unintentional.

This publication is not intended for use as a source of security, technical, legal, accounting, financial, or other professional advice. If advice concerning these matters is needed, seek the services of a qualified professional as this information is not a substitute for professional counsel. Neither the author nor the publisher accepts any responsibility or liability for your use of the ideas presented herein.

Some suggestions made in this book concerning business practices may have inadvertently introduced practices deemed unlawful in certain states, municipalities, or countries. You should be aware of the various laws governing your business practices in your particular industry and in your location.

While the Web sites referenced were personally reviewed by the author, there are no guarantees to their safety. Practice safe Internet surfing with current antivirus software and a browser with active security settings.

Dedication

As a salute to free enterprise, this book is dedicated to all of the security technology resellers who educate their customers on the product choices available, knowing that informed customers ultimately make the best decision for themselves, for their customers, and for the general economy.

Acknowledgements

I'm grateful to my fellow technology colleagues for their ideas and input. Whether it was a remark in passing, an axiom in an article, or a line from a speech, their thoughts and viewpoints enhance this book.

Heartfelt thanks to my business partner and best friend, Molly Leander for her unerring wisdom, gentle encouragement, and unending support. This book wouldn't be what it is without her.

Contents

TABLE OF CONTENTS

SECURITY

IN THE

BOARDROOM:

THE IMPACT OF PHYSICAL & NETWORK SECURITY ON CORPORATIONS AND WHAT EXECUTIVES NEED TO KNOW AND DO ABOUT IT.

INTRODUCTION

Companies are under attack from all sides, from the cyber world of the Internet and email, to the physical world of homes and offices.

While most companies of more than 1,000 employees have at least basic security policies in place, most small to mid-size companies have only made a cursory attempt at security. Executives and owners think, "We're too small. No one will bother us. Besides, we can't afford more security."

That may have been true in the past. No more. In 2004, the average small to mid-size business computer system was attacked more than seven times and nearly 59 percent of all computer security breaches were small business infiltrations.[1] Just 2.5 percent of the successful attacks were hits on big organizations.[2]

Industry analyst, Gartner[3] estimates that 70 percent of corporate break-ins are motivated by money or political reasons. The other 30 percent are random attacks to grab what ever unsecured assets are available and cash in on your hard work.

---

[1] Information Technology Solution Providers Alliance (ITSPA) survey. www.itspa.net

[2] London-based security firm, Mi2g, www.mi2g.com

[3] www.gartner.com

These perpetrators want to pilfer your proprietary property, cheat your customers, hinder your employees, and attack the heart of your business – your information systems and your vital physical assets.

The good news is that security technology is more affordable and more reliable than ever. The bad news is that the bad guys are more clever and vicious than ever.

Data Loss Costs

For most companies, their greatest assets after customer loyalty, are digital. According to a University of California study, 93 percent of information created by corporations is now in electronic form. Intellectual property is more than 70 percent of the market value of a typical U.S. company according to PriceWaterhouseCoopers.

It's a Big Deal

Estimated losses from computers not being operational in 2003 were US$18.2 billion up from US$11.8 billion in 1999.[4] If you lost your computer systems for even a few days or had key assets stolen, what would that mean to your operation?

Two out of five companies that experience an incident go out of business within five years. Businesses

---

[4]   See gbr.pepperdine.edu/033/dataloss.html for an article on financial losses from computer failure.

that can't recover within 24 hours have a 15 percent probability of failing and those who can't respond within 72 hours have a 40 percent failure rate.

A substantial number of companies close up shop after an attack because the average cost of computer downtime is more than US$50,000 per hour.[5] While your losses may not be that large, how many days could you survive? If you're operating on a razor-thin margin of one or two percent, just a few days could do you in.

Invaded in 20 Minutes

Now intruders come via the Internet. If you're connected, you'll be attacked. It's not a matter of if; it's a matter of when. And the *when* is coming sooner and sooner.

A recent study by the Internet Storm Center claimed that an *unpatched*[6] Windows® PC on the Internet will be compromised in less than 20 minutes.[7]

---

[5] www.contingencyplanningresearch.com/ 2001 Survey.pdf

[6] A *patch* is a bit of software that repairs flaws in the original program. Most programs need patches soon after release because the designers can't think of all of the ways that the program will be misused.

[7] When installing a new Windows PC that is connected to the Internet without firewall protection, infection is probable because the time to download critical patches exceeds the unprotected survival time. isc.sans.org

From the smallest operation to the largest corporation, critical business information is at risk. The route of attack could be as simple as a downloaded program from your kid surfing the Internet last night on the laptop that you're carrying into work today to connect to your corporate *server*.[8]

Protecting the Office

If you're office is like most, there isn't enough protection for your physical assets. A standard locking doorknob can be popped open with a pipe wrench in seconds. If you have fenced facilities, an attacker can cut through in 15 seconds, climb over with a ladder in five seconds, or crash through with a pickup truck in two seconds. Even austere measures like barbed razor wire can be circumvented in seconds with a piece of carpet.

In this book, you'll learn about what you can do to increase the physical security of your operation and protect your critical assets.

---

[8] A *server* is a computer used through a network (often simultaneously by many people) as compared with a desk-top machine usually used by one person at a time.

An Inside Job

Sadly, more than half of the successful theft and attacks on businesses come from disgruntled employees, fired staff, temporary workers, and opportunists.[9]

In a recent U.S. Secret Service report on computer attacks on banks, in 78 percent of the incidents, the attackers were authorized users with active computer accounts and in 43 percent of the cases they used their own *user name*[10] to carry out the incident.[11] I guess they wanted to get caught!

Simple procedures can eliminate most internal attacks, and in this book, you'll learn what those are.

Who This Book is For

This book is for executives of small to mid-size businesses who need basic to medium-level security.

If you're like most executives, computer and physical security aren't your areas of expertise, but because of legislation and business partner demands,

---

[9] For complete details on current cyber crime statistics, get the latest free report from the Computer Security Institute and FBI from www.gocsi.com.

[10] A *user name* is given to each person accessing a computer to uniquely identify them.

[11] www.cert.org/archive/pdf/bankfin040820.pdf
Insider Threat Study: Illicit Cyber Activity in the Banking and Finance Sector, August 2004.

you need to understand the security issues of your organization, your industry, and your competition.

This book was written with the non-technical executive in mind; it won't dig very deep into the technology. So, even if you have limited technical background, this book will give you a high-level introduction to security and guide you on the questions to ask and the issues to examine for your company.

Who's Responsible

Virtually every company that has been attacked had staff who knew they were vulnerable, but hadn't done anything about it. After the fact, they found out that they were responsible. Could you be in this position?

The courts have almost always made businesses responsible for the security of their customers and associated data. Legislators mandate corporate responsibility, and with it, more pernicious penalties for the executives involved. The bar is being set higher as to what constitutes *reasonable care*[12] in providing security for customers, employees, and their data. If there's a security breach in your company, you can count on being asked tough questions by your stakeholders and the law.

---

[12] A standard for determining legal duty, *reasonable care* is the attention that a reasonable person would exercise under the circumstance.

The responsibility for ensuring security in your company lies with you and your leadership team. The responsibility of putting security into practice lies with each member of your company.

If you have a contractual relationship with trading partners, consult your attorney. Some companies transfer liability in their contracts by expressly imposing liability for security breaches on vendors. Security liability may be governed by common-law contract principles, warranty, disclaimer and indemnification, and the Uniform Commercial Code.

The Executive and the Technology Committee

If you're like most executives, you're part of a technology purchasing committee that will also review security-related decisions.

Making technology decisions has never been easy. You have to slog through the marketing hype and jargon to separate the sales-copy promises from the product reality. If you're going to make smart decisions, you need to get answers to these security questions:

If you're a CEO, COO, President, or Owner – What are the threats to your organization? What are the risks and the costs of these threats? How are you personally liable? What would happen if critical business information or assets were compromised?

How do you direct the people who will lead your security efforts?

If you're a CFO or VP of Finance – What is the impact of security on corporate compliance and your cash flow? What do regulations demand from you? At what cost is it worth it?

If you're a CIO, CTO, or IT Manager – What are the risks to your computing infrastructure? How do you evaluate security vendors and solutions? What should you look for in a security vendor? How do you protect yourself and your organization?

Security as a Business Process

With the heightened concern for security and increasing legislation demanding it, your customers and vendors expect a secure environment and protection. So security has to become just as important as the trade secrets that keep you competitive.

When you make security part of your business processes, it's easy to illustrate that you're taking reasonable care in the event of a lawsuit, minimizing exposure.

In this book, you'll learn about the elements that make security part of your business process. Approach security with prudence and intelligence, and you'll outlast most attacks, directed or random.

Mitigating Risk

Risk can be thought of as a combination of three components:

Threat x Vulnerability x Financial Impact = Risk

Threat is the probability of a specific harmful event occurring. If the threat is improbable, such as being robbed by your loving grandmother, so is the risk.

Vulnerability is the probability of a particular threat causing harm. Security strategies decrease vulnerability and therefore risk.

Financial impact includes damage to assets along with wages and resources spent repairing damages. Soft costs include lost employee productivity, media damage control, a loss of public confidence, and lost business.

If a threat doesn't have much financial impact, such as an occasional petty theft, then the risk is low. Most businesses manage low-probability risk with insurance.

While threat, vulnerability, and financial impact matter, it's risk management and mitigation for which you're liable.

The Determined

There is no such thing as total security. If an attacker is determined enough, equipped well enough, financed well enough, or lucky enough, they'll succeed. So an important part of security is a solid recovery plan, discussed later.

If something happens, share information and don't point fingers. You'll create better security by sharing information with your trusted colleagues and reporting incidents to the authorities.

The Role of Law Enforcement

When you're attacked, either physically or electronically, immediately contact law enforcement officers. Most executives don't think about calling the police when their computer systems are compromised. Now, most police forces have cyber crime or computer crime units.

All United States federal law enforcement agencies investigate computer-based crimes.[13] Those with computer-specific taskforces include: the Federal Bureau of Investigation (FBI),[14] the U.S. Secret Service,[15] the U.S. Customs and Border Protection,[16] the

---

[13] A clearinghouse Web site with links and recommendations is www.cybercrime.gov

[14] www.fbi.gov

[15] www.secretservice.gov

[16] www.cbp.gov

U.S. Postal Inspection Service,[17] and the Bureau of Alcohol, Tobacco and Firearms.[18]

For example, the FBI is responsible for computer intrusion, identity theft, password trafficking, piracy of copyrighted materials and trade secrets, trademark and currency counterfeiting, Internet fraud and spam, Internet harassment, and bomb threats. The Internet Crime Complaint Center (IC3)[19] refers victims to the correct local, federal, or international law enforcement agencies.

The Moving Target

Threats come and go. Methods of mitigating risk change. The security market is moving so fast, that it's highly probable that by the time this book is in your hands, details will have changed, but the fundamental business-decision drivers won't change for several years, if not a decade.

Appendix A lists Web sites where you can get up-dated security information. Contact the leading manufacturers of security products to get the latest information about their products and business solutions. Many are referenced throughout this book and more are found with an Internet search.

---

[17] www.usps.com/postalinspectors

[18] www.atf.gov

[19] www.ic3.gov

A Word of Advice

Being influenced by a single manufacturer's sales rep results in myopic solutions and carries a high probability of less-than optimal results. I recommend that you select a competent, independent technology reseller who offers a range of products from a variety of vendors to be a part of your technology advisory team.

How to Use This Book

Start by scanning the first few chapters, stopping at the subheadings that catch your eye, to get a feeling for the elements of security. If you don't feel confident about a term, check the index for the first usage, where it is usually defined.

Review the case study that best matches your industry or your security situation.

Next, consider the assessment questions on page 108 to help explore the issues with your security committee.

Finally, select an independent technology reseller to help you make sense of the hundreds of security products available.

SECURITY PRINCIPLES

Security starts with deciding what you want to protect and then deciding how much you want to protect it. You don't want to protect everything; it's too expensive and annoys everybody.

Corporate security is about protecting your ability to conduct business, preserving valuable or critical assets that determine the well being of your organization. Your key assets are:

- People – your employees, customers, key vendors, and stakeholders.
- Property – physical, electronic, and intellectual.
- Processes – the procedures you use to successfully conduct business.
- Proprietary Data – trade secrets, confidential information, and personal data.

Security is about keeping *out* the bad guys who would misappropriate and misuse these assets, while letting *in* the good guys to appropriately use them to produce a profit.

What's Valuable?

Security is about identifying what is valuable and what requires protection. It's not logical to lock the lunch room, and leave the corporate database in a hall way.

The first step in your security plan is to identify what you can and can't live without. What are you legally required to protect? Defend this first, or you could go to jail. What do you need to operate your business? Defend that next, or you could go out of business. What is impossible to replace and what can be covered by insurance? What's a trade secret and what's common knowledge?

What's Vulnerable?

Security is about identifying vulnerabilities and threats to what's valuable, then minimizing or eliminating them.

It's about controlling the effects of equipment failure and human error. The good news is that protecting from malicious attack minimizes real-world mishap.

The Four Outcomes of Security

Solid security ensures continuous operation of your company by assuring *availability* of corporate assets, the *integrity* of those assets, the *confidentiality* of assets that are private, and making those who access the data *accountable* for their behavior.

1) Confidentiality

Your customers, employees, and vendors expect for you to keep their secrets. And if you handle your customer's money or keep a personal profile, legislation mandates information protection.

Security must limit access to only trusted people who need to use the data to serve the customer or do their job.

2) Integrity

If you're like most companies, every aspect of your business is managed and reported through your computer system. Your information *is* your company. Information integrity means that the data is accurate, up to date, and hasn't been corrupted or tampered with.[20]

In a physical sense, security prevents resources from being sabotaged or tampered with.

3) Availability

If your customers, employees, and vendors can't access the information and assets they need to do their job, you're out of business. Data and resources have to be available when and where your team needs them.

---

[20] For Symantec's tools on ensuring information integrity, see www.information-integrity.com

4) Accountability

All aspects of your security system must include unalterable audit trails so those who access your assets are held accountable for their actions.

Combining audited access with unique personal identification creates *non-repudiation*, or the ability for you to undeniably prove who did what. Non-repudiation is critical for successful security enforcement and prosecution of violators.

The Seven Layers of Security

There is no single way to protect your assets. Locks aren't enough. Alarms aren't enough. Guards aren't enough. The latest computer technology isn't enough. What's required is a *system* that includes some or all of the following elements, introduced here and discussed in-depth in later chapters.

1) Access Control

Control means letting users perform their authorized tasks, with authorized assets (including data), without being able to damage any of those assets. We want them to get in *when* and *where* they're authorized, whether it's access to the office in the morning or reading the daily operations reports from home. But we don't want them in the office at 3:00 a.m. when no one else is there.

Of course, authorized access shouldn't trigger alarms, but events should be recorded for auditing and accountability purposes.

2) Deter

The first line of defense in security is deterring the desire to target your assets. Most criminals are opportunists. When a crook recognizes that the risk of getting caught outweighs the reward of obtaining your asset, they'll move on. The higher the perceived threat of getting caught, the less valuable your secured assets become, and the greater the deterrence.

3) Detect

A resolute robber will attack your assets, so the security system must detect unauthorized activities, usually with an alarm system or a computer intrusion detection system. All detection technologies have limitations and don't detect every disturbance. The more layers of detection you have in place, the more likely an intruder will be intercepted.

4) Determine

When an alarm triggers, somebody must assess the appropriate reaction. Was it a false alarm caused by an insect crawling on the detector? Call the exterminator. Is an attacker hitting the corporate database? Terminate the session. Is an employee accessing an off-limits Web site? Filter the URL.[21] Is there more than one intruder? Dial 911.

In the past, a watchman, guard, or law enforcement officer assessed the situation. Now companies use video cameras to determine the correct action, dispatching the right response resources to the scene. Or a computer administrator receives details from the network surveillance system and notifies management.

5) Delay

If the intruder has gotten in, the security system needs to delay them long enough for the response force to arrive. If there is nothing to impede the intruder's access to your assets, such as a safe, internal locked doors, or complex password, then an alarm simply alerts you to a successful robbery. For example, if it takes two minutes for a crook to break in and grab the goods, and the cops show up seven minutes later, all they can do is file a report.

On this basis, most home security systems are merely a deterrent because they really don't secure anything other than a monthly income for the alarm company.

---

[21] *URL* (said U-R-L or erl) *Uniform Resource Locator*, the text address for a Web site that is translated into a numeric computer address for retrieval and display.

6) Defend

When an intrusion is successful, you must mount a defense. For the purpose of this book, the response force will be local law enforcement officers for physical attacks. For computer attacks, the response force will be your information technology (IT) expert.

7) Recover

If an intruder has been successful, you'll need to reverse the damage. In some cases, you'll be able to do so completely, but many times you won't be able to undo *all* the damage done.

If you've lost computer assets, you'll be able to restore the data and continue from your last back up point. If you've lost physical assets, your insurance agent will present you with a check and you can purchase replacements. If you've lost something unusual, you may need to hire a private detective to locate it or you may want to check on eBay.

Combine Layers to Increase Security

Now that you understand the seven layers of security, let's discuss how they combine to create varied security levels. This gives you insight into how you may approach security for your company.

Minimum Security

Found in most homes and some offices in low crime areas, this rudimentary level of security deters some unauthorized intrusion with basic barriers like windows and doors with simple locks. This will deter the average person or opportunist from gaining unauthorized access.

Low-level Security

Found in some offices and most homes in higher crime areas, this level of security deters and detects some unauthorized intrusion with reinforced doors or bars on windows and doors, high-security locks, security lighting, and a basic local alarm system. This will deter most casual crime, such as a thief looking for a quick US$50 for drugs.

Medium Security

Found in most companies that deal with high-value items, this level of security deters, detects, and assesses most intrusions and some unauthorized internal activity by using remotely-monitored alarms, or guards armed with a radio, cell phone, or a dog. This will deter most premeditated crime.

High-level Security

Found in organizations with valuable assets such as museums and banks, this level of security deters, detects, and assesses all intrusion and unauthorized activity using video monitoring, a perimeter alarm system, facility lighting, trained guards, and coordination with local law enforcement. This deters casual crime, most premeditated crime, and corporate espionage.

Maximum Security

Found in institutions where a security breach has serious social and environmental implications (such as prisons and nuclear facilities) this level of security deters, detects, assesses, and neutralizes all intrusion and unauthorized activity by using sophisticated, monitored alarms and on-site armed guards.

Security as a System

No single element of a security system is invulnerable because everything has a weakness and can be defeated. Guards can be bribed, knocked out, or distracted. Employees may succumb to *social engineering*.[22] Locks can be picked, jimmied, and keys stolen.

---

[22] *Social engineering* involves tricking a person into a behavior, like loading a malicious program. For example, an employee finds a disk labeled "Executive Salaries" in the parking lot. Curious, they put it in their machine, open the files, and inadvertently infect their computer and any unsecured machine on the network.

Barriers can be breached. Computer addresses can be *spoofed.*[23]

Intrusion detection systems are rated by the percent of *false positives* (false alarms) and the percent of *false negatives* (not detecting malicious activity). False positives put the response team into action unnecessarily and false negatives are a security hole.

While any method can fail, combinations of independent systems create higher exponentially higher levels of security. You can determine a complete system's protection level with *Bayes's Theorem* which calculates new probability based on a series of prior probabilities.[24] For example, if one system is 80 percent effective, then it fails one in five times. Bayes's theorem shows that two independent 80-percent-effective systems in series will fail once in 25 times for 96 percent effectiveness. Three will fail once in 125 times or 99.2 percent, quite secure.[25]

This means that you can use a series of inexpensive, independently ineffective measures that will add up to a tight security system. If the first layer doesn't catch them, the third or fifth one will.

---

[23] In security parlance, *spoof* means to counterfeit or deceive.

[24] *Bayes's Theorem* has implications in a number of situations from security, to finance, to theology. See plato.stanford.edu/entries/bayes-theorem for more.

[25] Bayes's Theorem (2[ed] form): $E^{total} = 1-((1-E^1)*(1-E^2)*(1-E^3)...)$ where E is the effectiveness of each system.

WHAT COULD HAPPEN?

Threats to your business come in many forms and can be classified in three areas:

- Natural Threats - Fire, flooding, mudslides, earthquake, snow and ice storms, volcanic eruption, tornado, high winds, hurricane, typhoon, epidemic, and tidal waves.
- Technical Threats - Power fluctuation or disruption, HVAC failure, gas leaks, water leaks, sewage leaks, and telecommunications failure.
- Human Threats - Robbery, burglary, vandalism, terrorism, sabotage, cracking, viruses, bomb threats, chemical spills, explosions, war, biological contamination, radiation contamination, hazardous waste, vehicle crash, backhoe digging in the wrong place, and work stoppage.

Likely Attackers

Let's look at the human threats that can be mitigated with security methods. People make premeditated attacks for three basic reasons: ideological cause, personal motive, or criminal intent.

Ideological Attackers

These people seek to do you harm because they see you as a philosophical enemy. They vehemently disagree with the values of your company and want you to stop. These people include terrorists, rights extremists, religious fanatics, militant activists, and foreign intelligence agencies. Their behavior can range from distracting to deadly.

Sometimes, ideological attackers come after companies that are part of the supply chain to an industry that they are targeting.

Personal Motive

These people are mad at you, your company, or your people, and they're plotting revenge. This group includes hostile terminated employees, disgruntled workers, resentful customers or vendors, and drug dependent and psychotic people.

Hostile Employees Attack

In most workplace crimes, the victim knows their attacker. An insurance industry study of workplace assailants found strangers perpetrated 16 percent of attacks, customers 36 percent, and current or former employees 43 percent. The victims were usually supervisors and domestic partners.[26] Remarkably, no studied attack was connected with corporate restructuring.

It seems the day of at-will employment is over. Now firing an employee brings with it the risk of backlash and lawsuit. The courts consistently find companies liable for protecting employees and customers from known perils.[27]

Preventing Employee Attacks

Nothing is a sure bet to eliminate an attack, but there are common sense things you can do to prevent them.

- Hit employee problems head on. Typical problem behaviors: conflict with others, poor performance, misuse of sick leave, chronic tardiness or leaving early, and unfounded complaints. When you see this conduct, intervene *immediately*.
- If the employee doesn't respond, the old proverb, "hire slow, fire fast," serves well. Terminate them before they build an irrational grievance. Document your actions to defend your position in court if necessary.
- Workplace assailants sometimes make their plans clear. Take seriously subtle and overt threats of

---

[26] www.noworkviolence.com is one source of ideas for avoiding workplace violence.

[27] As quoted in a report from the National Security Institute at nsi.org/Tips/workdeth.txt

violence. Document them and turn the case over to the police.

- Train employees to report suspicious behavior. Create an anonymous reporting system to encourage action.
- Report all crimes by employees or ex-employees, such as vandalism, stalking or harassment, verbal threats, or assaults.
- Alert your staff about newly terminated employees. Make a clear policy to never allow a dismissed employee access to your office or premises.
- Control security codes, passwords, and keys so that dismissed employees don't have access to any assets. More about this on page 49.

Conduct Employee Background Checks

Screening employees is more important than ever because most crime is an inside job. Due diligence includes background checks.

Some companies have found that one-third of all applications received included a major fabrication, and 90 percent of the applicants with criminal records didn't admit it.

Negligent hiring and retention laws in at least 28 states hold employers liable for employee misconduct and the average settlement is US$1.6 million.[28]

---

[28] www.liabilityconsultants.com

You can deter many marginal job applicants by posting a simple sign reading, "If you do drugs, don't apply. We conduct full background checks."

Considering how much it costs to select and train an employee, a background check is worth the investment. If you don't want to do the background check yourself, there are agencies who will conduct the search for you. Look in your yellow pages under *private investigators* or *detective services* or look on the Web.

Ask your attorney for the correct wording on your job application to authorize the background check.

What's Sensitive?

If your competitor could use it to create an advantage, you need to protect it. The theft could be by an employee courted by a competitor. Only permit access to corporate secrets to people with a need-to-know.

Have your attorney review employment contracts to ensure that you have strong legal remedies if an employee leaves with company property.

What's Easily Stolen and Sold?

Thieves target anything that can be grabbed, stuffed into a briefcase or computer bag, and quickly converted into cash. For example, audio visual equipment, computers, DVDs, and CDs. Employee background checks and escorting visitors help prevent these thefts.

Most laptop computers and corporate A/V equipment feature a *security slot* ready to connect to a security cable. Use these to tie down valuable equipment, deterring opportunists.[29]

Criminals

These people will attack for economic gain, such as theft, ransom, or extortion. Criminals can be part of an organized racket, lone perpetrators, opportunistic white collar workers, or they may act on the behalf of a competitor.

Is it Hacker or Cracker?

A *cracker* (as in safe cracker) intentionally breaches computer security for profit, malice, for personal cause (a *hacktivist*), or just for the challenge. Some crackers claim they're only identifying security system weaknesses. Few law abiding souls buy that excuse.

A *hacker* is a hands-on computer programmer with an aptitude for creating clever code. Often journalists incorrectly refer to a person who attacks computer systems as a hacker.[30]

---

[29] www.kensington.com

[30] Perhaps it's because in some parts of the country *cracker* insults their audience.

A cracker is usually not a brilliant hacker, but a mediocre programmer using common tricks to exploit well-know weaknesses.

Random intrusions come from *script kiddies* with little technical knowledge. They use widely-available tools and scripted procedures that target well-known vulnerabilities. Defense against these attackers is simply keeping software updated.

Criminal Computer Attacks

At one time, computer attackers were malcontents seeking notoriety, launching vendettas or vandalizing weakly-secured Web sites, always leaving evidence of their escapades. Now attackers are motivated by money, sending *spam*[31] to steal identity,[32] or pitch products and services, legal and illegal. Common offerings are pornography and gambling.

---

[31] *Spam* is unsolicited commercial email. *SPAM* (all uppercase) is the 1937 trademark for a meat product from Hormel Foods that is most popular in Hawaii. Someday your kid might ask, "Why did they name this stuff after junk mail?" I'm sure you'll have a snappy answer ready.

[32] Details on page 35.

CAN-SPAM[33] legislation, designed to limit spam in the U.S., hasn't worked. Sophisticated computer farms churn out millions of messages a day from countries with non-existent anti-spam legislation, circumventing investigation and prosecution. A worldwide problem, 90 percent of email messages are spam or contain a virus according to Malte Pollmann, Lycos Europe director of communication services.

---

[33] The *Controlling the Assault of Non-Solicited Pornography and Marketing* Act of 2003. Apparently the U.S. Congress views pornography and marketing as equivalent threats.

ARE YOUR COMPUTERS CRIMINALS?

A bigger problem is co-opted corporate and personal computers that mass mail unbeknownst to the owner. About 70 percent of the spam intercepted by MessageLabs[34] in 2004 came from computers infected with a *virus, trojan,* or *worm,* collectively known as malicious software, or *malware.*

Virus Strikes

A computer virus secretly attaches to an email or another computer program, often altering the program. It can be malevolent, destroying files, or benign, popping up a greeting. It spreads when passed to other computers by unaware users who don't follow safe computing practices.

Trojan Invasion

Like the legendary wooden horse used by the Greek army during the siege of Troy to trick and defeat a better situated army, a trojan is malicious computer

---

[34] www.messagelabs.com

code disguised as a desirable utility, game, or file sharing tool. It reports back to its creator and can take control of the victim's computer.

Silent Worms

Now more common than viruses, a computer worm is malicious code that does no harm to the host, but secretly invades and takes over the computer to do the nefarious bidding of its creator, like a *zombie*. A worm silently propagates through network and Internet connections. They try to remain invisible and are often only noticed when the infected computer slows to a crawl or when an antivirus scan detects it.

Backdoor Key

A worm often installs a *backdoor*, code that allows unauthorized access through the network, also called a *remote access trojan (RAT)*. This means that an attacker can do anything they wish with the computer, such as update the worm to fix bugs or take command of the computer zombie.

Zombie Computers Arise

These zombies form a *botnet*, a network of clandestinely controlled computers sending spammer's emails or leveling other attacks.[35] In 2004, broadband

---

[35] See www.messagelabs.com/emailthreats/intelligence/ reports/monthlies/October04 for more on botnets.

provider Comcast found that infected subscribers sent more than 800 million emails per day.[36]

Denial of Service

Botnets are used to launch a *directed denial of service (DDoS)* attack on a Web site or email server. A botnet bombards the target site with Web page requests or spam, overloading the server, making it unavailable for legitimate users, called *denial of service (DoS)*. Think of DDoS as creating a computer busy signal.

Harvesting Email Addresses

Botnets can launch *directory harvest attacks (DHA)* to gather email addresses. Spammers direct messages at a company using a dictionary of common email names, collecting addresses that aren't rejected. A successful attack nets thousands of fresh addresses in minutes. That's why you can establish a new email box and almost instantly get spam.

During a DHA or DDoS attack, your email service slows substantially, inhibiting legitimate message delivery because the email server responds to each message sent to an unrecognized address.[37]

---

[36] www.senderbase.com

[37] Sing with your best Elvis impression, "Return to sender, address unknown..."

I See What You're Doing

Spyware secretly collects and reports user behavior like Internet surfing habits, keystrokes, or system activity. It can scan computer systems and steal information like financial data, passwords, employee identity, or trade secrets.[38]

Most spyware automatically installs and runs without the user's knowledge. Infections occur by visiting a Web site with an insecure browser, come as part of a trojan, or even by viewing an on-line video. Malicious spyware easily infiltrates computer security because it comes from a user-requested Web site.[39]

Eight out of 10 computers are infected by some form of spyware.[40] Business users identify spyware as the fourth-greatest security threat.[41]

Spyware can degrade computer performance and impact employee productivity with pop-up advertisements and application crashes. Dell executives claim that spyware accounts for 15 percent of support calls.

---

[38] One fascinating site on spyware: www.benedelman.org

[39] Common spyware includes Alexa, Cydoor, Ebates Precision Time, Claria/GAIN/Gator, WhenU, VX2, 2020 Search, iWon, 180Solutions, and Ibis Toolbar.

[40] A study co-sponsored by America Online and the National Cyber Security Alliance. www.staysafeonline.info/news/safety_study_v04.pdf

[41] www.idc.com

"Legit" spyware admits to covert surveillance deep in the user license's legal mumbo jumbo.[42] Because the user agreed to the license and thus, the intrusion, the software isn't usually classified or detected as a virus.

Customer Identity Theft

The fastest growing criminal scheme is ID theft, now a US$100 billion problem. Identity theft is directly related to drug trafficking, money laundering, and terrorism. As much as 70 percent of all identity theft starts with an employee stealing personal data from the company.[43] Organized crime appears to be driving ID theft; it's relatively safe for the criminal and highly profitable. For example, racketeers take jobs as bank tellers to steal customer identity.[44]

This means that you need to protect sensitive customer information. Indeed, legislation demands that you do. For example, the Sarbanes-Oxley Act[45] defines records retention and corporate governance, Gramm-

---

[42] For example, Precision Time is an application that updates the computer clock, a standard feature in Windows XP, and spies on the user.

[43] *Identity Theft* for the National Institute of Justice, J.M. Collins & S.K. Hoffman, 2002 January

[44] www.occ.treas.gov/ftp/alert/2002-4.txt

[45] www.sarbanes-oxley.com

Leach-Bliley Act[46] and the Data Protection Act in the United Kingdom[47] demand control of personal information, and the Health Insurance Portability and Accountability Act (HIPAA)[48] spells out behaviors for healthcare providers and others.

Most legislation includes draconian penalties of fines and prison time for the officers of offending companies. These days, ROI means risk of incarceration.

How to Protect Your Customers Against Identity Theft

- Conduct background checks on employees who handle personal information. Limit what information temporary and new employees can access.
- Never use Social Security numbers (SSN) for employee and customer identification. Require that your vendors not use SSNs for identification.
- Train employees how to collect personal information from customers to ensure security. For example, clerks shouldn't ask for private data in a busy store.
- Don't ask for more personal information than is necessary or appropriate. Doing so opens you to unnecessary risk.

---

[46] www.ftc.gov/privacy/glbact/
[47] www.legislation.org.uk
[48] www.hipaa.org

- Secure all employee and customer personal data whether in filing cabinets or in a database.
- Train your staff on security policies about releasing personal data by phone, fax, or email. Have them obtain written permission by verifiable means.
- Use paper shredders at each workstation to destroy sensitive data. Enforce a policy for destruction of discarded CD-ROMs, computer hard disks, and tapes. You may wish to consider using a secure document destruction company that may be cheaper than buying shredders for all.

How to Protect Yourself from Identity Theft

A name and Social Security number, a pre-approved credit application,[49] canceled check, bank record, or any document containing personal information fished from the trash is enough for a criminal to pose as you and tap your creditworthiness.

It may take months for the results of identity theft to show up as unusual bills or a bad credit rating.[50]

A regular credit report review is essential to detecting identity fraud. Contact the major credit

---

[49] Call 888-5-OPT-OUT to opt out of credit reporting bureaus' mailing lists for pre-approved credit offers.
[50] PrivacyRights.org is a good source for ID theft information.

bureaus for a copy of your credit report.[51] Everyone is entitled to one free credit report annually as of September, 2005.[52] Follow these guidelines:

- Never leave mail in your mailbox overnight. Deposit outgoing letters in a locked mail box or at the post office and retrieve items from your mailbox immediately after delivery.

- Shred unwanted documents with personal information before discarding.

- Never give personal information over the telephone or the Internet unless you initiated the contact and you're certain that you're talking with an authorized employee. If in doubt, hang up and call the main number obtained from the phone book or directory assistance.

- Don't offer more information than is appropriate. For example, your doctor doesn't need your driver's license number. Just because an application asks for your SSN doesn't mean that you need to comply.

---

[51]   Equifax, (800) 525-6285, www.equifax.com
Experian, (888) 397-3742, www.experian.com
Innovis, (800) 540-2505, www.innovis.com
TransUnion, (800) 680-7289, www.tuc.com

[52]   www.annualcreditreport.com is operated by the three major credit bureaus to facilitate this federal mandate.

Who to Call for Help

- Call the police. A copy of the police report proves the crime to creditors.
- Call any one of the three major credit bureaus and ask them to place a *fraud alert* on your file. Upon confirming the fraud alert, the other credit bureaus are notified automatically.[53]
- If the U.S. Mail is involved, call your local Postal Inspection Service office.[54]
- File a complaint with the Federal Trade Commission.[55] The FTC offers detailed information on ID theft recovery.
- Close any account that was fraudulently opened or used.
- If fraudulent bank accounts were opened, contact check-guarantee companies to reject any written checks.[56]

Business Identity Theft

Experts feel that soon business identity theft losses will dwarf personal ID losses.[57] Your corporate credit

---

[53] Equifax Fraud Unit: (888) 766-0008
Experian Fraud Unit: (888) 397-3742
TransUnion Fraud Unit: (877) IDTHEFT

[54] www.usps.com/ncsc/locators/find-is.html

[55] www.ftc.gov or www.consumer.gov/idtheft

[56] See a list of check guarantee companies on page 131.

lines are much larger. When many people access the corporate checkbook or credit card accounts, fraud may not be discovered if there isn't a watchdog monitoring transactions. Deceit is difficult to detect when working with a large number of checks and charges from a wide range of locations.

Protecting Your Bank Accounts

Guard common business information, such as banking information and tax ID numbers.

In Colorado, seven crooks were convicted for stealing business bank account numbers to forge payroll checks. In Florida, three temporary employees stole bank account numbers to create counterfeit checks.

A Michigan business owner of 25 years discovered he was the victim of business identity theft when the Small Business Administration (SBA) informed him that he defaulted on a US$480,000 loan. A criminal simply used his federal employer identification number (FEIN) to obtain the loan.

Stealing Your Identity

What's worse is when attackers impersonate your business to steal your reputation and your customers.

---

[57] See *Business Identity Theft* by Judith M. Collins, www.auditnet.org/articles/jfa-collins.pdf

The owner of a New York company received more than US$24,000 in yellow pages bills for an ad using their business name and address but someone else's phone number.

Internet Impersonation

Business impersonation on the Internet is called *phishing*[58] or *brand spoofing*. Phishers use fake email messages purportedly from a legitimate business and counterfeit Web pages to con that business's customers in to disclosing personal and financial information.

This isn't just the scam of sophisticated crooks. Reputed *phishing kits* downloaded from the Internet do all the Web page coding and spamming automatically making phishing accessible to anyone.

Big Phish

According to the antivirus company Sophos, spammers send hundreds of thousands of phishing e-mails daily.[59] Gartner reported 57 million adults received phishing e-mails in 2004, of which 11 million clicked through, and 1.78 million provided passwords and

---

[58] Pronounced *fishing*. Like angling with artificial lures, although most fish won't bite, some will take the bait.

[59] www.sophos.com

personal information resulting in fraud losses of US$2.4 billion.[60]

The Anti-Phishing Working Group (APWG) reports that unique phishing attacks have been growing at 110 percent per month and as many as five percent of recipients divulge personal information.[61] eBay has more than 800 people on staff just to deal with business identity theft.[62]

Phishing Inside

Phishers can trick employees into giving up corporate passwords. After launching a directory harvest attack, a phisher fakes a message from IT asking users to verify their passwords.

The secret to avoiding this is a clear password and personal information disclosure policy.

Phishing by Mail

Phishing isn't restricted to email. Be wary of letters or phone calls requesting additional sensitive information connected with a recent publicly recorded event, such as real estate transaction or corporate filing.

Call your original service provider to verify any request for information.

---

[60] www.gartner.com

[61] www.antiphishing.org

[62] www.cfo.com/article.cfm/3013867

Throw Back the Phish

- Educate employees to never provide confidential information and to never click on links in unsolicited email. If someone has been phished, forward the e-mail to uce@ftc.gov and call the FTC help line, (877) FTC-HELP.
- Avoid phishing by educating customers about how you'll use their information, how you'll contact them, and what questions will be asked. For example, America On-line has included this warning on chat windows for years: "Reminder: AOL will never ask for your password or billing information."
- Watch for phishing attacks by assigning someone to monitor for fraudulent email.[63] Set up a specific email address[64] to which customers and employees can forward suspicious emails purportedly from your company.
- Consider investing in an online fraud management solution from a vendor like Symantec.[65]

Been Phished?

If your company has been the target of Internet fraud, waste not a moment and hit the problem head on.

---

[63] See survey.mailfrontier.com/survey/quiztest.htm for a quiz and instruction on how to spot phish fraud.

[64] Such as spoof@yourcompany.com

[65] ses.symantec.com/onlinefraud

- Contact the local FBI office or FBI Internet Fraud Complaint Center and the Federal Trade Commission.[66]
- Email all of your customers and prospects acknowledging the attack with suggestions on how to deal with it.
- If a fraudulent Web site is involved, have your IT department demand that the host ISP delete the site.

New Check Fraud

Identity theft doesn't just mean scamming a credit card number (you're only liable for the first US$50, if anything), checking accounts can be cleaned out. The Check 21 Law[67] which permits conversion of paper checks to digital images makes this rip-off easy.

After phishing access to a victim's bank account, the criminal retrieves check images and monthly statements. They counterfeit virtually identical checks including the signature and unused check numbers, and cash them for a reasonable amount based on information gleaned from the monthly statements, circumventing fraud detection schemes. The bogus check is scanned and shredded by the bank as

---

[66] www.fbi.gov, www.ifccfbi.gov, and www.ftc.gov
[67] www.federalreserve.gov/paymentsystems/
truncation/faqs.htm

{ 44 }

permitted by Check 21, eradicating all evidence of evildoing.

Ask your banker how they will protect you from this kind of fraud.

Instant Messaging = Instant Mess

Instant messaging (IM) or *chat* connects people whether they're at their desktop or in the field with their cell phone or personal information device. It facilitates rapid communication with minimal cost. Industry analyst META Group puts official corporate instant messaging at 17 percent, while according to Sybari Software, unsanctioned usage exceeds 90 percent.[68]

Yet without security mechanisms in place, it's an open conduit for confidential files, malicious code, and improper content. Symantec claims an IM virus could infect half a million users in 30 seconds.

Wireless Messaging

Wireless messaging opens additional security holes. For example, an attacker can use a stolen cell phone to impersonate the user, requesting sensitive information that probably will be readily disclosed. If mandates require corporate communication archives, you have no control over where or how long wireless text messages are stored.

---

[68] www.sybari.ws

Securing Instant Messaging

IM is almost impossible to forbid, so either adopt this as a business tool with specific policies for IM usage and security, or block it completely.

The best solution is to use industrial-strength IM software with built-in protection, such as IBM's Lotus Workplace Messaging.[69] Or increase security with these tactics:

- Configure your antivirus software to protect IM against attack.
- Only allow IM within your organization, or with secure vendors or customers.
- Disable file transfer services to defeat viruses and protect against unauthorized file transfer.
- Block messages with key words like project names.
- Establish message archives to meet regulations and create audit reports to meet compliance requirements.[70]
- Create policy to never disclose sensitive information via wireless messaging.

Hoax Email

Virus hoax warning emails often describe impossible virus characteristics and dire consequences. With

---

[69] www.lotus.com

[70] One company that does this is FaceTime Communications, www.facetime.com

capitalized copy and copious exclamation points, they claim "THIS ISN'T A HOAX!!!" It often quotes a semi-credible person, "I'm worried it could be bad." Forwarded from multiple senders, it implores you to email it to every friend and colleague.

Some hoaxes describe how to detect infection and delete the offending file (typically a critical system file) disabling the computer. So, hoax emails become a destructive virus when a user takes naïve action and then forwards it with their endorsement, "I found this file on my computer and I may have infected you!"

Don't forward email that meets the above criteria, and certainly don't follow any included advice.[71]

Attack Through Outside Vendors

If your vendors connect to your computer systems, you have a potential security issue. Consider these ways to minimize your exposure:

- Create performance contracts that spell out how they'll interface with you and what security standards they'll maintain.
- Many companies create vendor portals that require a user name and password to secure access.
- Discuss business continuance plans with critical vendors. If they're attacked and shut down, what

---

[71] See a list of hoax-busting Web sites on page 127.

will that do to your business? How will you respond?

- Investigate their hiring practices and how they
  conduct employee background checks. Limit access by subcontractors who may be a security risk.
- Ask your attorney about creating contractual
  indemnities and liability exceptions.

ACCESS CONTROL TACTICS

Access control combines three elements *authentication,* *authorization,* and *accounting,* collectively called *AAA.*

Authentication

The first step to access control is verifying that a person is who they claim to be. If an attacker can't get past the authentication system, they can't do damage.

Authenticate by confirming *something you know* such as a lock combination or a password; *something you have* such as a key or ID card; or *something you are or do* such as physical attributes or behaviors.

Something You Know

A password is the oldest and simplest way to identify friend or foe; just ask a question that only an authorized person can answer.

For example, financial institutions ask for your Social Security number, your mother's maiden name, or a *personal identification number (PIN).*

You may use combination locks, where the person has to remember the number sequence to gain access.

Passwords

Your first line of defense against unauthorized access is a combination of user names and passwords, allowing authentication of individuals and providing a rudimentary level of non-repudiation.

Passwords can be defeated by:

- The user disclosing to another their user name and password.[72]
- It being observed as it was typed in (called *shoulder surfing*).
- Being found on a cheat sheet near the computer.
- Being discovered by attackers with a *dictionary attack* or *brute force attack*.[73]

Internal and External Passwords

When you access external systems or Web sites, your user name and password are often open to interception. For this reason, create policy to always use different user names and passwords for internal systems that are never used with external systems.

---

[72] In a recent public survey, 71 percent revealed their password to a complete stranger and 40 percent knew a colleague's password. www.securitypipeline.com

[73] Widely-available tools such as *crack* and *11oft* attempt to bypass log-in systems by trying frequently-used passwords from a dictionary, then resort to brute force by trying all other letter and number combinations.

Complex Passwords

Complex passwords are created by mixing upper and lower case characters, numbers, and special characters to create a password that can't be found in a dictionary (like o0iCu812).[74] An eight character password like this generates 6,095 trillion possible combinations; you're pretty safe.

While they're complicated to crack, they can be unreasonable for users to remember. Each month, about 30 percent[75] of passwords are forgotten and manually reset by help desk personnel, with the greatest number on Mondays and after a holiday.

If users can't remember passwords, then they'll write them down. The more often that a user is forced to change their password, the more likely they'll write it down.

Do a quick audit in your office; find out how many people have a sticky note with passwords on their monitor, hidden under their keyboard, or sitting in the top desk drawer. You'll be surprised.

Create Memorable Complex Passwords

You can create a complex password by using the first letter of each word in a memorable sentence. For

---

[74] A classic complex password, this one happens to be in attackers' dictionaries.

[75] Industry survey numbers range from 15 to 40 percent.

example, "I love to ski and dive but not at the same time," yields Il2s&dbN@tst.

You can also create a complex password by simply typing in a short sentence. Another method is alternating the characters of two words into a single password. For example, blend *milk* and *eggs* to create the password MeIgLgKs.[76]

Simple Passwords

Simple passwords, like a four-digit PIN, are easy for users to remember. While easy to crack, a short password is very secure when your system locks out a user name after a small number of log-in attempts.

Password Policy

Consider the following tactics for creating secure passwords:

- Set policy that access to all personal computers requires a password.[77]
- Strictly prohibit users from giving others their password. Create guest accounts with very limited capability for casual users or visitors.
- Permit passwords that are simple to remember, but not the company name, user name, or other password that's easily guessed by a colleague.[78]

---

[76] Or to make an omelet.

[77] Most experts suggest changing passwords regularly. I don't see the point if you use the rest of these tactics.

- Lock out a user name after four sequential failed attempts to prevent password cracking attacks.

- For network access, only permit a user name to be logged on in one location. This enforces not sharing user names.

- Use complex passwords for your servers and critical computers. Better yet, use stronger, two-factor authentication, discussed on page 55.

- Train users how to create complex passwords that they can remember but are hard to crack.

- Train users to choose different user names and passwords for external systems and Web sites to prevent internal access information from being accidentally disclosed.

- You may choose to require that laptops have complex passwords at start up, securing the data if the computer is stolen.

- Use a screen-blanking[79] screen saver with a simple password (one comes with Windows) to secure an un-occupied computer from an inside attacker. While rebooting easily defeats a screen saver, the attacker will have to re-log on to the computer with a password.

---

[78] The most common passwords are *admin* and *password*. Most passwords are the names of pets, sports teams, children, and family members.

[79] A blank screen saves energy and makes the computer appear to be off, further deterring internal attack.

- A computer that's off is quite secure, so switch off workstations on weekends and holidays. Consider shutting them down at night.[80] This doesn't apply to corporate servers.

Single Sign-on

Single sign-on permits a user to be authenticated once to access multiple authorized applications. It eliminates future authentication prompts during that session when the user switches applications.

Single sign-on eliminates inconsistent password implementation between applications, keeps the password count to a bare minimum, makes it easy to authorize or un-authorize a user, and saves time logging in and out. Single sign-on vendors include Citrix,[81] Enterasys,[82] IBM Tivoli,[83] Oracle,[84] and RSA.[85]

Something You Have

Another way of verifying a person is by an article in their possession, such as an ID card or key. A unique item delivers a higher level of non-repudiation.

---

[80] Most experts now agree that turning off a PC extends its life and delivers a 60 percent energy savings. The concern about damage on power-up just isn't valid.

[81] www.citrix.com

[82] www.enterasys.com

[83] www.tivoli.com

[84] www.oracle.com

[85] www.rsasecurity.com

Two-factor Authentication

Article-based authentication can be easily circumvented if the item is stolen or borrowed, so it's frequently used with a second method, creating *two-factor authentication*.

For example, a signed credit card (an article) and a matching signature (a behavior) allow a clerk to authorize a charge.[86] Or an ID badge (an article) with a photograph (a physical characteristic) gains access via a guard. Or your ATM card (an article) and your PIN (a password) gets cash for lunch.

Security Token

A security (or authentication) *token* is a small device such as a *smart card*,[87] a key fob, or *USB device*[88] that uniquely identifies a user to the security system.

The most secure tokens become part of the user's guarded personal possessions, like their wallet for a

---

[86] Payment processing guru, Dan Alcorn calls a family member's unauthorized credit card use *loving fraud*, as the victim refuses to prosecute the perpetrator.

[87] A *smart card* is a credit-card size device embedded with a data-filled microchip. Some require physical contact with a reading device, others can be queried remotely. More than a billion are used world wide. One vendor is RSA Security.

[88] A *Universal Serial Bus (USB)* device plugs into most modern PCs, making it easy to transport between computers.

card or keys for a fob. If not, the token may be left behind, becoming useless to the user and potentially useful to the finder.

Security tokens are often part of a two-factor authentication system with a user name or PIN that identifies the user as the owner of that specific device.

For example, RSA's SecurID gives users a key fob or credit-card size device that displays a new six-digit code every 60 seconds. To log on, users enter the code along with their user name and password. RSA now offers a system for Microsoft Windows as an alternate to static passwords.[89]

VeriSign offers their Unified Authentication managed service using USB devices. They manage the verification and infrastructure.[90]

Secure Computing offers a SafeWord token that generates a one-time password on each touch of the device's button that's combined with a user name and PIN to authenticate access.[91]

Controlling the Keys

Secure physical assets with a lock and key. But the security is only as strong as the lock and as safe as the people you trust with the key. Commonly-held keys

---

[89]   www.rsasecurity.com

[90]   www.verisign.com

[91]   www.securecomputing.com

have a very low non-repudiation level, so if you want auditable behavior, don't trust keys alone.

Some tactics to increase key security:

- Check keys in and out. Have employees sign for each key and only give them a key if it's necessary to perform a daily task.
- Invest in high security locks available only from locksmiths with keys that aren't easily duplicated at the corner store. Mark them "Do not duplicate."
- If you have standard locks, re-key critical locks upon employee termination.
- Don't put identifying marks on keys. Never put your name, address, or phone number on keys. Better to replace keys then have them returned by a thief, in person, at night.

Something You Are

The authentication method with the highest level of non-repudiation is based on who you are. *Biometrics* uniquely identify someone by measuring and analyzing unique human body characteristics such as fingerprints, eye retinas and irises, voice and face recognition, hand geometry, and even DNA matching.

Biometrics is going main stream as IBM offers ThinkPad laptop computers with a built-in fingerprint reader that replaces user passwords. Door locks with fingerprint readers can be had for less than US$500.

Authorization

Authorization permits what a user can do. It enforces policies by allowing or disallowing the users' activities and privileges with resources, services, and data. Authorization can be set up by job function with a view to a user's roles and responsibilities.

For example, you may allow an accounting department employee access to financial records from their desktop during normal business hours, but disallow access with their user name from other machines or outside business hours. If they need to work after hours, you can set up a one-time user name and password to accommodate them, yet retain strong authorization control.

Another example, you may wish to allow a supervisor to view the files of their direct reports, but not make changes nor view the files of other supervisor's employees.

Access to the highest level of authorization should be restricted to people who you trust completely, and should still be audited. As good policy, only allow top level access for the task at hand, logging in with lower authorization for routine tasks. The highest levels of authorization may require two people to gain access.[92]

---

[92] An extreme example, launching a U.S. ICBM requires two operators to simultaneously turn keys at independent workstations.

Accounting

Accounting measures the resources consumed during access (such as computer system time used and how many data transactions occurred) supplying usage details for departmental or customer billing, and trend analysis for growth forecasts. Accounting also can monitor activity and track unauthorized access attempts, a behavior that is grounds for dismissal at many companies.

AAA Servers

A dedicated *AAA server* often delivers authentication, authorization, and accounting services. Most use the Remote Authentication Dial-In User Service (RADIUS) standard that maintains a central database of user profiles shared by all other servers. This makes it easy to enforce access policy. For example, a single change to the AAA server database ends all computer access to a terminated employee.

AAA server vendors include Citrix,[93] Computer Associates,[94] Cisco,[95] HP,[96] and IBM Tivoli.[97]

---

[93]   www.citrix.com

[94]   www.ca.com

[95]   www.cisco.com

[96]   www.hp.com

[97]   www.tivoli.com

Deterrence Tactics

Deterrence is about convincing a would-be attacker that the risk of being caught is higher than the reward of their unauthorized actions.

Advertise Your Armor

Robbers pass up houses with barking dogs; they don't want to get bit. Banks have seen a 36 percent decrease in robberies just by posting a "No Hats, No Hoods, No Sunglasses" sign. This policy makes crooks easier to identify, so discourages robbery.

Warning that you're on guard deters most casual crooks and makes professional criminals think twice.

You can:

- State your security policies on your Web site
- Post signs notifying of alarm systems
- Post signs notifying of video surveillance
- Post signs that criminal activity is vigorously prosecuted.

While you want to announce capabilities and intentions, keep the details secret.

Light It Up

Simply increasing the level of lighting around your business reduces crime from 10 to 85 percent. Retail customer surveys consistently find that well-lit locations draw more business than poorly-lit ones. So, increasing light levels may help business, too.

Consider high intensity discharge (HID) lamps such as a long-life high-pressure sodium vapor lamp that delivers efficient bright white lighting.[98]

You're On Camera

Cameras are useful for intrusion detection and invaluable for situation assessment.

Video cameras provide a strong deterrent; video evidence is compelling. Just posting notice that the area is monitored discourages attackers.

Dummy cameras have long been used as an effective deterrent, but they have a downside. If there is an occurrence in an area that people believe is monitored, they may assume that help is coming.

Covert cameras are legal for surveillance in many circumstances but usage should be reviewed by your attorney. It's generally improper to put a camera where people expect privacy, such as bathrooms and locker rooms.

---

[98] www.osram.com

Put Your Name On It

Your mom did it when you were in school, and you should still do it. Attach permanent asset tags to equipment making them less desirable to steal and easier to identify if they are stolen.

Close and Lock Doors and Windows

Deterrence is also about locking doors and windows, both physical and in cyber space. Consider these tactics for securing your physical assets.

- Create a closing procedure checklist, ensuring all assets are secured at the end of the business day.
- Control keys as discussed on page 56.
- Each employee has their own alarm code so that access outside of business hours can be audited.
- Managers review all alarm access reports.

Update the Operating System

Older computer *operating systems*[99] such as Windows 95 and 98 are full of security holes and have got to go.

---

[99] The *operating system (OS)* is the base-layer software that interfaces the hardware (display, keyboard, disk drives, central processing unit, memory, and so forth) with the software that runs your business. This lets software designers ignore the hardware and focus on the functions that you want. When you *boot up* your computer, the system loads the OS so that you can then run your business applications.

Get the latest version of Windows and download the latest security patches. Consult your IT expert on updates. There are regular cases where a new patch creates more problems than it fixes.

Sign up for Microsoft Security Update, a free e-mail alert service designed for small businesses that tells you what to do and when to do it.[100]

Warning Window Closing

The time between the announcement of a security hole and an operating system exploit is shrinking. When Microsoft releases a service pack for Windows, crackers compare old and new code, then engineer malicious exploits targeting unpatched computers.

According to security provider Symantec, an exploit now emerges less than six days after a vulnerability announcement.

Ultimately, an intruder will launch an attack the same day that the vulnerability is discovered, called a *zero day exploit*.

Choose a Different Operating System

Every major virus, worm, and trojan released in 2004 targeted Microsoft Windows security flaws, with little impact on other operating systems such as BSD, Linux, Mac OS X, and UNIX.

---

[100] www.microsoft.com/security

You may wish to choose a different operating system to avoid the Microsoft-targeted attacks.[101]

Computer Security Depends on Your Operators

A computer operator can intentionally or inadvertently remove security safeguards on any operating system and open it up to attack. Most system administrators who have experienced a security breach knew that they were vulnerable and hadn't done anything about it.

True for any system, your operators need to know what they're doing and follow established guidelines on configuring the computer to meet your required level of security.[102]

Updating Applications

Many commonly used computer programs or business applications have security holes. Even seemingly invulnerable programs, like RealNetworks' RealPlayer[103] have been hit. Make sure that the latest

---

[101] See my book, *Linux in the Boardroom: How Linux is Changing Corporate Computing and What Executives Need to Know and Do About It* for an executive-level discussion on choosing an operating system.

[102] For a series of articles on stupid security mistakes, see searchenterpriselinux.techtarget.com/qna/ 0,289202,sid39_gci962066,00.html

[103] www.service.real.com/help/faq/security/

program patches are installed and that security settings are set to maximum level. This is especially true of Microsoft office applications.[104]

Protecting Your Secrets

Encryption provides a high level of security for sensitive data like financial transactions or trade secrets.

Encryption converts data into *ciphertext* that appears meaningless. *Decryption* converts encrypted data into *plaintext,* a readable format. To read the message, the receiving person must know how to decrypt it.

There are a wide variety of encryption techniques available. Choosing which method depends on your needs. For many companies, widely-used *pretty good privacy (PGP)* is efficient and sufficient.[105]

Encryption offers these characteristics:

- Confidentiality - the information can't be viewed by unintended recipients.
- Integrity - any information alteration is obvious because it won't decode into meaningful text.
- Authentication - the sender and receiver can confirm each other's identity and the validity of the message.
- Non-repudiation - the sender can't later claim that they didn't create the message.

---

[104] office.microsoft.com/officeupdate

[105] See web.mit.edu/network/pgp.html or www.pgp.com

Hardening Hardware

Protecting your physical resources requires just a little common sense: lock up critical resources, lock down computer hardware.[106] But there's more to it.

Stolen Equipment

What if an attacker steals a piece of equipment? What if it's your laptop with next year's confidential plans? What if it was taken by a competitor at a trade show? (Their excuse if caught, "I'm sorry, I thought it was mine. I have a laptop just like it.")

Protect your critical information these ways:

- Never list passwords in a file on your computer.
- Always encrypt all critical information.
- As an alternative, don't carry critical information on your computer. Instead, leave it on a secure server and access it through the Internet.[107]
- Back up your critical files every day to an offsite location. You take your deposits to the bank every day; make the same consideration for your valuable data.

Are You Throwing That Away?

The FBI estimates that information theft costs U.S. businesses up to US$100 billion annually. Much of

---

[106] Discussed on page 27.

[107] One vendor, Citrix offers complete solutions of this type. www.citrix.com

this is from competitors dumpster diving for confidential reports that should have been shredded.

Place cross-cut shredders at workstations where employees handle and discard confidential information. If you're not going to shred, at least lock up the trash.

Physically destroy the hard disks of any computers you dispose. Or ask your IT people to make sure that they're completely wiped clean using a utility such as Symantec's Wipe Info that's part of their Norton SystemWorks® package. Completely eliminating Windows data can be tricky, so follow the directions carefully.

Destroy CD-ROMs and DVDs containing obsolete back-up data. A shredder that turns a disk into chips in two seconds costs less than US$50.

Secure Web Transactions

Most Web browsers support *SSL encryption*[108] to securely transmit data over the Internet. The browser and Web server automatically perform the encryption and decryption.

When the Web address you're viewing starts with *https://...* (instead of *http://...*) you know the browser is using SSL to securely transfer data. SSL doesn't

---

[108] Secure Sockets Layer (SSL) describes how the data is passed through *sockets* between computers and applications. Just know SSL means secure.

guarantee that the Web site is safe, just that the data is encrypted during transmission.

Secure Communication with the Office

A *virtual private network* (*VPN*) provides secure access to your company network through the Internet. A *private network* uses costly leased phone lines to securely transmit data. A VPN provides virtually the same capability, without the expense.

Unlike a private network, you can setup a VPN connection anywhere you can access the Internet. VPNs encrypt data before sending it through the network, securing it from attackers.

VPN vendors include Checkpoint, Cisco, Enterasys, Juniper Networks, SafeNet, SonicWALL, Symantec, and Watchguard.

If you want your people to access company confidential data through a wireless network or while traveling, require a VPN or SSL Web access and use SSL-based email servers.

Walling in Wireless

The odds are good that you have a *wireless network*[109] in your company, either sanctioned or secret.

---

[109] *Wireless networks* known as *Wi-Fi* or 802.11 connect computers and the Internet with radio links.

And why not? Wireless networking equipment is cheap and it's tempting to cut the cord and access the network from anywhere.

But widely available tools let attackers monitor or transmit data on your wireless network. They can intercept emails, snag files, and take command of your Internet connection.

If your wireless network operates with the default settings, you're wide open. Consider these methods to close and lock the wireless window:

- Change the wireless network password. Attackers try *admin* first because it's the default password used by all major vendors.

- Disable administration from a wireless connection so that an attacker can't take control of your connection if they guess your password.

- Change your *service set identifier (SSID)* to something that doesn't identify your company.

- Better yet, if possible turn off SSID making your network invisible to most scanners.

- Turn on *wired equivalent privacy (WEP)*. This weak encryption may discourage casual attackers but it's not secure for business use.

- Better yet, get a wireless network device with *Wi-Fi Protected Access (WPA)*, providing much stronger encryption and authentication.[110]
- Select who gets on the network with *MAC address*-based filtering.[111] Of course, this makes your wireless network unavailable to casual users wanting to log on with their own, un-secure computer, but that's not a bad thing.
- Update your wireless network software because manufacturers continuously repair problems, patch security holes, and add new features.
- Place your wireless network antenna in the middle of your service area, minimizing the signal outside your perimeter. Some wireless networks can adjust the radio power; choose the lowest level that works.
- Screen critical wireless areas to reduce signal leakage. For example, Force Field Wireless makes a window film and paint with copper and aluminum that stops radio waves.[112]

---

[110] Check Point's Safe@Office is one wireless security device with these capabilities.
www.checkpoint.com/products/safe@office
[111] The *Media Access Control (MAC) address* is a unique serial number built in to each computer or network device used to determine where messages come from and where replies should go.
[112] www.forcefieldwireless.com

- Assume that public Wi-Fi networks are not secure. If you choose to retrieve email over public networks, use a VPN or log on to a secure Web server with SSL encryption.

Safe Internet Connection

In the cyber world, a *firewall*[113] is the interface between your private network and the wild, wild Internet. The firewall hides computer addresses from outsiders and blocks unexpected and unsanctioned traffic between your network and the Internet. Most security vendors offer a firewall solution.

Hardware Firewalls a Must

If you connect to the Internet, you must have a hardware firewall or you will be compromised. Hardware firewalls can also guard against viruses, block spyware, and defend against some DoS attacks. Firewalls can be a standalone box or built into a network router or other network *appliance*.[114]

---

[113] A *firewall* in the physical world is a fireproof or fire-resistant wall that prevents the spread of fire through a building or a vehicle.

[114] An *appliance* is a computer-based tool designed to perform a specific function, usually for less cost or more securely then with a computer and software.

Hardware firewall vendors include Checkpoint, Cisco, Enterasys, Juniper Networks, SafeNet, SonicWALL, Symantec, and Watchguard.

Software Firewalls Secondary

Software firewalls[115] should be a secondary line of defense. They are more vulnerable than a hardware firewall because they can be disabled by a user or by some malware. Many attacks come through a browsed Web site, and by then it's too late for a software firewall to act. Software firewalls work better to detect unexpected outbound traffic from a computer.

Safer Internet Connection

A *proxy server* is an intermediary computer between users' computers and the Internet that controls and enforces security policy. It checks the users' request against content filtering and access policy, forwards the request to the Internet hiding the user's identity, and logs the activity. Like a firewall, proxy servers prohibit unauthorized access from the Internet to the internal network.

Proxy servers speed up Internet access by keeping copies of frequently accessed Web pages in a *cache* (a

---

[115] For example, BlackICE, MacAfee Firewall, Norton Firewall, ZoneAlarm, and the firewall shipped with Windows.

local memory), rapidly delivering the local copy when the page is requested.

Safest Internet Connection

A *DMZ* (*demilitarized zone*[116]) is a computer or small network between a company's private network and the Internet. The public can access the DMZ computer, for example to get data or a Web page, but can't get to the private network. A DMZ is a more secure than just a firewall and can act as a proxy server.

Protecting Mobile Devices

Mobile phones, smart phones,[117] and *PDAs*[118] make life on the road so much easier. But confidential information gets stored on these devices with virtually no security. Gartner estimates that 90 percent of mobile devices aren't secure.

For example, is your CLIÉ®, iPAQ®, or Palm® set up with a sign-on password? If not, anyone who finds it or steals it has all the data they need to pretend

---

[116] The term comes from the geographic buffer zone established between North and South Korea following the early 1950s UN action.

[117] Such as the RIM Blackberry.®

[118] A *Personal Digital Assistant* is a handheld computing device used for email, calendaring, and address books, and other applications. Most feature wireless connections.

they're you. Have you stored passwords, credit card, or banking information? You're compromised. Do you access your corporate database with it? Then your PDA is an attacker's ticket in.

Mobile devices that use *Bluetooth*[119] can connect with another Bluetooth device within 30 feet, creating a potential security risk. If you have a Bluetooth device, select the *undiscoverable*[120] mode to hide your device, and turn it off if you're not using it.

Secure your mobile devices with these tips:

- Protect your PDA with a log-in password. It's the least you can do!
- Put your phone number on the outside of the device. If you lose it, an honest soul who finds it can contact you even if they can't get past the password.
- Synchronize (or back up) your PDA before you leave the office so you won't lose valuable data.
- Install the latest operating system patches, increasing security.
- Virus writers now target PDAs. Get virus protection if you use your PDA to access the Web or communicate with email.[121]

---

[119] *Bluetooth* is a short-range wireless standard designed to eliminate wires between devices.
[120] In this mode, you can communicate with other devices but must initiate contact.
[121] See www.symantec.com for antivirus solutions.

- Don't leave your PDA lying around. Put it away in your pocket, bag, or drawer.
- Set policy on what can and can't be stored on a PDA or mobile phone and audit occasionally. Insist on encryption of sensitive corporate data.
- If you use your PDA to access the corporate network, use a secure VPN tool to ensure data security.[122]
- Consider using a mobile device security management tool like Credent's Mobile Guardian.[123]

Other Data Leaks

That oh-so-cool iPod® can be a security risk. A simple connection to the company computer's USB or *FireWire*[124] port turns it into a disk drive, ready to suck in corporate secrets.

A USB drive the size of your thumb can quickly siphon away a gigabyte of confidential documents or upload a backdoor trojan.

Slip a CD into the burner and walk away with the corporate customer database.

---

[122] www.checkpoint.com, www.cisco.com, and others offer solutions.

[123] www.credant.com

[124] *FireWire*, Apple Computers version of standard IEEE1394, is a high speed connection between a computer and external devices, like disk drives.

Consider a third-party security solution like SmartLine's DeviceLock® that centrally controls which Windows users can access USB and FireWire ports, Wi-Fi and Bluetooth adapters, CD-ROMs, floppy drives, other removable devices.[125]

Forwarding Sensitive Data

Users might email an unfinished project to themselves so they can retrieve and complete it on their home computer. But their less-secure home computer creates an exposure risk.

Implement policy that prohibits company data from being on home computers, or require that any computer used for corporate data meets the company's security policy.

Inside Protection

What if a salesperson calling on your company wants to plug into your network to access the Web, send email, or print a document? How do you ensure that their laptop won't infect the network or open a security hole? What if it's one of your employees with a personal laptop?

Consider tools that inspect every computer connecting to your internal network to ensure that it meets security policy and is clean of malware.[126]

---

[125] www.protect-me.com

[126] www.checkpoint.com/products/interspect

Control What's on the Computers

If your policy demands that only sanctioned software can run on company computers, you can conduct a *software audit* for prohibited applications and files or for compliance with security settings.

A software audit can also compare the software licenses you own to the actual number installed, managing software license liabilities and cost.

Control What's on Your Network

Web filtering or *content filtering* controls personal Internet access, limits unwanted content on your network such as pornography, music downloads, and unsanctioned programs, and can increase security from Web-based threats.[127]

How Secure Are You?

Assessing vulnerability helps you understand what you need to secure and prioritize security tasks.[128]

Penetration testing often uses the same approach as a real attacker to expose vulnerabilities. The tester, sometimes called an *ethical hacker,* reports findings and suggests steps to supplement security.

---

[127] SonicWALL is one vendor of content filtering appliances. www.sonicwall.com

[128] eEye offers tools to do this. www.eeye.com

Another approach is *passive vulnerability assessment,* which observes normal network traffic to assess risk.

The two approaches compliment each other, as penetration testing is invasive and costly, and passive testing can run continuously.

DETECTION TACTICS

Detection is about discovering unauthorized activity and triggering a response, such as an alarm or a defensive reaction.

Detecting Malware

Every computer must have antivirus software that searches for known or potential viruses. Antivirus software also scans incoming emails, Web pages, and instant messages for malware and, if found, deletes or quarantines it to be dealt with later. Most antivirus programs use *heuristics*, sensing malware based on malicious behavior, and *signatures*, detecting viruses based on how the virus was created.

Most antivirus packages automatically update every few days with new definitions because of the number of threats that emerge each month. Leading antivirus vendors are McAfee, Symantec (Norton), and TrendMicro.

If you suspect your computer is infected with a virus you should scan with HouseCall, TrendMicro's free, online virus scanner.[129]

---

[129] housecall.trendmicro.com

Detecting Computer Spies

Various tools help detect and remove spyware. Like antivirus tools, they must be regularly updated as the bad guys figure out new ways to sneak a peek.

Software solutions have to be installed on each computer. Examples include LavaSoft's Ad-Aware,[130] CA's PestPatrol®,[131] McAfee's AntiSpyware.[132]

Hardware solutions can watch everyone on the network. For example, Check Point Software Technologies includes anti-spyware capabilities in its VPN-1 device.[133] TippingPoint Technologies offers spyware protection in its UnityOne intrusion-prevention system.[134]

Detecting Email Threats

Scanning email to detect spam, viruses, and unsanctioned messages can be done by the email server at an individual computer, or outsourced to a service company. Centralized or outsourced email scanning makes sense if you choose to enforce email policy or if you're mandated to archive company messages.

McAfee, Symantec, TrendMicro, and others offer software email scanners. Hardware solutions come

---

[130] www.lavasoft.com

[131] www.pestpatrol.com

[132] www.mcafee.com

[133] www.checkpoint.com

[134] www.tippingpoint.com

from Chapache, Mirapoint, SurfControl, and others. Outsource vendors include MessageLabs and Postini.

Detecting Network Intrusions

Network *intrusion detection systems (IDS)* observe network traffic for potential attackers. IDS can be performed with software[135] or as a network appliance.

If you have to protect valuable assets, consider using both methods because each is capable of detecting events that would be difficult or impossible for the other to identify. Typically, an intrusion triggers an operator alert to take action.

An *intrusion prevention system (IPS)* can take immediate action when an intrusion is detected, for example blocking specific network traffic upon detecting a malicious action.[136]

Detecting Physical Intrusion

Classic intrusion detection techniques include door and window switches, motion detectors, and pressure sensors.

Intrusion detection can set off a local alarm or can report to a central monitoring facility. Whichever you

---

[135] See www.snort.org for free, community supported IDS software.
[136] One vendor, Enterasys, calls there solution Dynamic Intrusion Response. www.enterasys.com

choose, make sure that a response team can arrive soon enough after the alarm to stop the intrusion.

If you want to use video cameras for intrusion detection, instead of hiring a guard to watch a video screen, choose digital video processing that can detect motion and can trigger an alarm. Humans aren't good intrusion detectors because their ability to detect a disturbance degrades after 30 minutes and becomes unreliable after 60 minutes.[137]

---

[137] As cited in *The Design and Evaluation of Physical Protection Systems*, Mary Lynn Garcia, Butterworth Heinemann, 2001.

ASSESSMENT TACTICS

When an alarm sounds, the situation must be assessed to determine how to take action. Is the alarm valid or was it a false alarm? If the alarm is valid, what needs to happen next?

There are several methods to assess an intrusion. You could go look, you could dispatch a guard, or call local law enforcement. Or you could use a video camera.

Video Surveillance

Video cameras are excellent to assess a situation. A guard can view the video and make an instant decision what to do next and record the video for future review and potential criminal prosecution.[138]

Cameras have some drawbacks. They require careful configuration to ensure optimum image quality. Outdoor cameras need special attention to account for changing weather conditions. Cameras need protection against overt tampering or destruc-

---

[138] Check with your attorney on video evidence requirements for successful prosecution.

{ 83 }

tion and may need protection against covert tampering, such as a substitute video feed.[139]

Local TV

Closed-circuit television (CCTV) uses hard-wired analog cameras, cables, recorders, and TV monitors. Currently found in extensive surveillance operations, they have limited suitability in small business as door access monitoring.

They are limited by cabling length restrictions (typically 3,000 feet) and have restricted video quality. They are also labor intensive because video tapes have to be changed daily.

Digital TV

IP cameras[140] (also called *network cameras*) are digital video cameras that connect to the computer network. Instead of generating a video signal, these cameras produce *JPEG files*[141] that can be accessed, monitored, recorded, and printed anywhere on the network by

---

[139] The movie, *Ocean's 11* (2001 version) uses both of these methods to circumvent the casino cameras.

[140] *Internet Protocol (IP)* describes that the camera can connect to a standard network. A leading vendor is Sony. www.sony.com/onsite

[141] *JPEG* (said jay-pehg) is the *Joint Photographic Experts Group* which defines digital picture compression methods and standards for picture files.

an authorized user. The image resolution is usually much higher than analog cameras.

The cameras connect to the network with a standard network cable or wirelessly with Wi-Fi. One server with a single software application runs the entire system and any authorized user has direct access to any camera.[142] Or the camera can send video to multiple destinations.

Adding cameras is easy; just plug another into the network. Adding more recording time is easy; just add another disk drive to the camera server.

If you plan to use more then a few cameras, you'll want a dedicated network because cameras can produce a lot of data, slowing down other corporate network traffic.

Smart Cameras

Some cameras have a built-in activity detector that can set off an alarm, turn on more light, and email or upload images to a server.

Because the camera continuously analyzes and stores the images, it can show the events that lead up to the trigger.

Some cameras can connect to traditional alarm sensors, enhancing detection.

---

[142] For a cool example, see www.camerawebpage.com

Point and Shoot

IP cameras are frequently mounted on *pan-tilt-zoom (PTZ)* heads controlled through the network. They can be pointed and directed by any authorized user from anywhere on the network.

Event Analysis

Cameras can be triggered to record by normal events, such as a cash-register drawer opening. Software applications let your security experts analyze specific events, like every time a clerk makes a transaction of more than US$500.[143]

This means that you can locate and prosecute events that employees thought went undetected.

---

[143] www.verintsystems.com

DELAY TACTICS

Once the alarm has been raised, the environment needs to delay the attacker long enough for forces to arrive to catch them red handed.

In this sense, delay is not about using physical force to detain an attacker. Leave that to the experts who carry weapons.

Physical Delay

In the physical world, this means that you alarm the perimeter of your facilities, and place your most valuable assets in a strong room, or at least behind walls and doors that are resistant to assault. The attacker will be delayed and detained getting through the doors and walls. If the attacker thinks it will take too long to reach their objective, they will abandon the attack.

Cracking the Safe

You may choose to use a safe for your most valuable assets, delaying the attacker further. There are two primary types of safes; the *fire-resistant safe* and the *burglary-resistant safe*. If you want to protect an asset from both the fire and theft, security experts recommend placing a fire-resistant box inside a burglary-resistant safe or purchase a fire-rated burglary safe.

A fire-resistant safe keeps the contents cool enough to not be consumed by a fire. They are made of materials that don't conduct heat and are suitable for documents. If you intend to store computer media, such as disks, tapes, and CD or DVD-ROMs, make sure that the safe is rated for them, as these items are much more sensitive to heat when compared with paper. Fire-resistant safes aren't designed to thwart a determined thief.

Burglary-resistant safes are designed to thwart picking, drilling, and cutting. The days of a safe cracker listening to the tumblers are over, as modern safes use locking methods that don't make noises. These safes are designed to keep items that can survive heat away from a thief.

Cyber Detainment

In the cyber world, those who wish to detain an attacker set up a *honeypot*, a server whose sole purpose is to catch an attacker.

For example, the Symantec Decoy Server creates a realistic mock network environment as an attack target in order to protect critical areas of the network. It acts as an early warning and detection system to divert and confine attacks.

DEFENSE TACTICS

In the cyber world, the attacker probably resides in another country, so there's not much you can physically do other than pull the plug on the network and rebuild it with new defense mechanisms.

In the physical world, the best response for a small to mid-size business is to call the local law enforcement officers when you're notified of an incident. Consider meeting with them to discuss emergency response plans and to have them audit your physical security policy or advise and evaluate your requirements.

Emergency Action Plan

Create a specific response plan that you can enact when an emergency arises. The U.S. Occupational Safety and Health Administration (OSHA) offers tools to help small, low-hazard service or retail businesses create an emergency action plan and comply with OSHA's emergency standards. The plan doesn't create a legal obligation.[144]

---

[144] www.osha.gov/SLTC/etools/evacuation

Fire Extinguishers

One physical defensive action you can take against fire is with a portable extinguisher. Portable extinguishers can put out fires before the sprinkler system activates, avoiding water all over your computers, furniture, and carpets.

The National Association of Fire Equipment Distributors found that hand-operated fire extinguishers put out more than 90 percent of reported fires in commercial facilities.[145] In most cases, the fire was completely extinguished before the fire department arrived.

For computer systems, choose a gas-based class C fire extinguisher that's suitable for electrical equipment. These use carbon dioxide or one of the Halon replacements such as Halotron.[146]

As an alternative, there are dry powder extinguishers that use non-corrosive potassium bicarbonate (called Purple K). It cleans up with a vacuum or by sweeping.

Consult your fire department on extinguisher selection because using the wrong type of extinguisher can make certain types of fire worse. Many fire departments also schedule regular extinguisher safety inspections.

---

[145] www.nafed.org

[146] www.halotron-inc.com

DISASTER RECOVERY TACTICS

A *disaster recovery plan (DRP)* and a *business continuity plan (BCP)* describe how an organization deals with disasters and outlines how to keep the business running during the recovery

Business continuity is a proactive plan that keeps a business up and running after a disaster or failure, or better yet, prevents failures all together by minimizing their effects. A typical plan includes an alternate computing site with a current copy of the corporate database and a means to switch over operations when disaster strikes.

Disaster recovery is a reactive plan that requires time and money to restore operations. Ideally, critical data is available at a failover site and then you'll rebuild the systems as quickly as possible.

Your Disaster Recovery Plan

A disaster recovery plan includes precautions to minimize the effects of a disaster. Appropriate plans vary from one business to another, depending on variables like the type of business, the business processes, and the level of security needed. It is not unusual for a larger company to spend 25 percent of its IT budget on disaster recovery.

Part of your recovery plan must address the impact of a disaster on your supply chain. What happens if a critical vendor is attacked?

For a list of sample plans, see the Disaster Recovery Journal's Web site.[147] It includes a questionnaire that you can use to assess the DRP of your important vendors.

The bibliography on page 132 lists several excellent books on disaster recovery and contingency planning.

---

[147] www.drj.com

THE BUSINESS CASE FOR SECURITY

When you buy a security solution, you're buying insurance. The business case for security is based on avoiding costs associated with loss and legal exposure.

The Costs of a Security Breach

If you're successfully attacked, there's going to be a mess to clean up, whether it's sweeping up broken glass or issuing everyone new user names and passwords. Some of the cost factors are easy to calculate, others are much fuzzier.

Direct Costs

This is what you'll pay out to undo the damage. Depending on the disaster, it can range from a few dollars to closing down the company. Here are some of the potential costs:

- The cost of lost intellectual assets such as custom software and the cost to recreate lost, corrupted, or deleted data.
- The cost of replacing lost physical assets such as equipment, supplies, and your physical plant.

- The cost of cleaning up and repairing the damage. Emergency repairs often cost more.
- Cost of notifying customers of breach of confidential information.[148]
- Cost of public relations to reposition the event in your favor.
- The costs of educating employees, customers, and vendors about the breach and how to prevent recurrence.
- Costs of communicating with shareholders, explaining what happened and what you're going to do about it.
- The cost of legal actions. What is the legal exposure because you cannot fulfill contractual or mandated obligations?

Indirect Costs

These are costs that you'll incur in the form of unrealized business, the money you would have gotten if the breach hadn't happened.

- Lost present business. How much will your company lose, per hour, if you are struck by disaster? Look for internal and external interdepend-

---

[148] Concerned with ID theft, California's Database Security Breach Notification Act (SB1386) requires that customers be notified if a company believes a computer system's breach has compromised the personal information of any California customer.

encies between your business processes and those of your customers and vendors.

- Lost future business. What does it cost when you can't respond to a customer or prospect request? Your customers may require you to implement new levels of security or demand new service level agreements before they re-extend their business to you.
- Lost competitive edge. What happens to your market position if your facilities are struck by disaster?
- Loss from negative public relations. A negative story about you becomes positive marketing for your competition.
- Shareholder lost confidence. What happens to the value of stock when shareholders lose confidence?
- Lost employee productivity during restoration.

The Costs of Security

These are the costs associated with preventing a future intrusion and avoiding the direct and indirect costs of an attack.

This is a partial list of general costs to implementing a security solution:

- Staff training for those unfamiliar with security. Calculate wages, overhead, and training costs for on-line training. Add travel expenses if you select classroom-based training.
- Researching security vendors.

- Evaluating solution options.
- Purchase of security elements.
- On-going maintenance support for security hardware and software.
- Required security management and reporting tools.
- Migration costs, including testing of the new system.
- Costs of inefficiencies introduced by the security policies and systems.

The Value of Security

This is a partial list of general savings from implementing a security solution:

- Increased staff efficiencies from not having to individually deal with security issues, like spam and viruses.
- Increases in efficiency created by the security system because of upgraded technology.
- Eliminated cost of security breaches from unpatched software.
- Reduced business interruptions caused by security breaches.
- Reduced legal exposure from unsecured premises and computer systems.
- Incremental sales based on your improved security and stability.

Running the Numbers

It's difficult to create *return on investment (ROI)*[149] numbers that satisfy everyone. In some cases, you may just want to avoid another attack; forget measuring ROI, just don't let it happen again. Or a business partner may demand a higher level of security, and you're planning to mark up your services to cover the costs.

One way to establish the value of a security solution is to calculate the system's *reduction in loss* (sounds like an oxymoron) by taking the difference of the average annual loss expectancy with and without mitigation.

Loss reduction =
Loss without mitigation – Loss with mitigation

The amount of loss reduction is the most you should spend on mitigation. Frankly, some losses aren't worth insuring against.

The value of the security solution is the difference between the cost to mitigate and the loss reduction provided by mitigation.

Value of mitigation =
Cost of mitigation – Loss reduction

---

[149] Sometimes called Return on Security Investments (ROSI).

Repeat the calculation for each component of your security system to determine your overall ROI.

The challenge to these calculations is coming up with the probability and cost of a threat, and the reduction of risk by a specific security solution.

Historical data can suggest the likelihood of a specific threat. Losses can be estimated by the costs to repair the damage, the costs of idle employees, and estimated business loss.

YOUR SECURITY STRATEGY

Every company faces the same fundamental security issues; the security vulnerability list released by the FBI and Computer Security Institute does not frequently change. What changes from company to company is the philosophy.

Most companies take a head-in-the-sand, oh-it-won't-happen-to-us approach. Fewer companies have a policy, but inconsistent enforcement. Even fewer companies have a strong security policy that's part of the corporate culture. How will you approach security?

Where Do You Want to Go?

The process of updating security in your company is similar to bringing on any other new technology. Break up the task into manageable chunks and just get started on the most important pieces.

Begin by reviewing what level of security you need. Then identify the barriers to making that happen. Next, assemble a committee to craft strategic approaches to eliminating the barriers and evaluate potential solutions. Create smart questions that uncover the necessary information so that you can make intelligent choices, balancing risk and reward.

Security strategy is based on *policy, education, technology, measurement,* and *enforcement.*

Security Policy

A *policy* is a document that summarizes requirements and prioritizes expectations that *must* be met for specific areas of the company. It details what's authorized, what's unauthorized, when policies apply, and who is responsible for maintaining and enforcing the policies.

For example, an *acceptable use* policy covers regulations for using corporate resources, such as computers, phone systems, company vehicles, and other physical resources.[150]

A *standard* is a specific technical requirement that must be met by everyone. For example, a computer must be in a specific, secure configuration before connecting to the corporate network. Following industry standards provides a level of indemnification when a contract demands reasonable care.[151]

A *guideline* is a recommended best practice that becomes established through experience. Effective security policies use existing standards and guide-

---

[150] Enterasys makes an acceptable use policy solution for networks. www.enterasys.com

[151] Consult your attorney.

lines. This speeds adoption, because it capitalizes on the corporate culture.

Corporate Security Policies

Policy must cover legal liability issues such as security liability, privacy, disabled-person access, and training. Physical security policy documents employees' right to privacy, prohibitions such as drugs, alcohol, and weapons, and use of force by employees and guards.

It also must cover failure to protect issues like embezzlement, exposure of trade secrets, and compromised employee or customer data. Include appropriate legislative requirements such as Sarbanes-Oxley Act, Gramm-Leach-Bliley Act, and HIPAA.

Many of these items should be covered in your standard employment contract so that you can enforce policy.

Regularly review and update policies when there are major changes to legislation or your operations.

Get Started

Start by creating a policy that defines roles and responsibilities. It's easier to write and approve a three page document than a 200-page tome. Keep it short and focused, assigning responsibility to the right people and moving implementation details to the right level of expertise.

Classic policy details scope, reasons, definitions, domains, roles and responsibilities, management, documentation, implementation, measurement, and updates and changes.

Sample Policies

A quick Web search of "sample security policies" turns up a number of free and for fee examples.

SANS offers sample security policies developed by a group of experienced professionals; a good starting point.[152]

The IT security policy for Murdoch University in Australia is a tight document covering the key points, including permission for use by others.[153]

The *SAFE Blueprint* from Cisco Systems[154] is a best-practices technical discussion about business computer networks. It takes a defense-in-depth approach so the failure of one security system won't compromise the rest of the network. Although the recommendations are product agnostic, the solutions center on products from Cisco and partners.

---

[152] www.sans.org/resources/policies

[153] wwwits2.murdoch.edu.au/security/policy.html

[154] Cisco Systems is a major computer networking vendor. Get details at www.cisco.com/go/safe

An expensive but widely regarded book, *Information Security Policies Made Easy* includes electronic templates and fully-developed examples.[155]

Education

The biggest bang for your security buck is educating your people because it puts security into action. Educate all employees and vendors about your security procedures and consequences of non-compliance. Yes, this costs money, but so does insurance and your legal team. Some managers complain, "If I train them, they'll just leave." Well, what if you don't train them, and they stay?

Security breaches begin with, "I don't have to worry about my password; I only use the network for printing."

Most education is simple, like reminding employees to not discuss sensitive procedures with outsiders. Teach them that security is a group responsibility; a chain is only as strong as its weakest link.

Training ROI

Measure the impact of the training. Use these five criteria:

- Did you like it? This comes from the end-of-session feedback.

---

[155] www.pentasafe.com

- Did you remember it? Discover this with reviews, quizzes, and tests.
- Did you use it? Learn this from observation, follow-up feedback, and occasional audits.
- Did it work? Have supervisors report in on the training effectiveness.
- Was it worth it? Combine all of these elements to measure the training ROI.

Overcoming Cultural Resistance

Organizations with effective security inculcate the strategy into company culture. Insist that every supervisor, manager, and executive follow security procedures, leading by example. One executive believing that they're exempt from the rules can defeat your security policy.

If you're making major changes to corporate culture, you'll meet resistance. Plan for it and use these tactics to move through it:

- Empathize with the discomfort and difficulty of change.
- Emphasize the necessity for the new approach.
- Elaborate on the value of compliance and the costs of non-compliance. Personally recruit the diehards to lead the charge.
- Be willing to replace resistant people. Better to retire a 20-year veteran because they refuse to change than close the company because of a serious security situation.

- Chunk the training into short weekly sessions instead of longer sessions occasionally. This allows for material review and compliance check with peers.

Measurement

It makes no sense to have a policy that's not measurable because no one knows how well they're doing or where they need to improve.

Some things are easy to measure, for example you can survey who's wearing an ID badge and who isn't. Other things are more difficult to measure, such as who's carrying home unauthorized confidential documents.

Software tools can measure company-wide security policy compliance and can tell you how secure you are.[156] Many of these tools come pre-configured with security policies based on standards and best practices, making policy easy to implement and measure.

Audits

Regularly audit access to confidential information to determine how vulnerable you are. Review what information is accessible, by whom, and where and how it is accessible.

---

[156] One widely-regarded tool is Symantec's Enterprise Security Manager. www.symantec.com

Enforcement

Few people want to play the heavy in enforcing security policy. Yet, a policy without enforcement is a set up for major trouble.

Rules and polices don't have the force of law. You can't physically detain someone because they broke a corporate rule unless it's backed up by legislation. But you can dismiss them.

One of the easiest ways to enforce policy is to make security compliance part of the regular performance review process. A good worker who isn't safe isn't good for your company.

Devise a series of warnings with increasingly stiff sanctions. Some infractions need to carry the penalty of instant dismissal, such as committing felonies on company property. You may wish to create rigorous responses to seemingly minor security infractions if those lapses result in legal exposure.

If an employee, vendor, or customer breaks the law, call law enforcement.

Do it In-House or Outsource?

Do you choose to staff your security team internally or use outside managed services?

Your internal team certainly understands your business and operating procedures, but probably doesn't have the background and skills to implement a full security solution.

On the other hand, a consultant may understand the security world, but may require time to understand how to implement security without unduly impacting your operation.

Managed security services (MSS) deliver an expert and systematic approach to security. You can expect services such as around-the-clock monitoring and managing intrusion detection systems and firewalls, overseeing patch management and upgrades, performing security assessments and audits, and responding to emergencies.

A good solution for many small to mid-size businesses is to take a blended approach. Identify what you can do yourself, training users and growing internal security expertise. Use outside vendors and managed services to cover complex and technical details that don't change much from company to company and don't interfere with your operation, such as network management.

Getting Help

Before hiring a security solution provider, learn more about their ability to deliver.

The company should have a Certified Information Systems Security Professional (CISSP) on staff. This industry certification requires passing an extensive test and providing proof of experience. A good alternative is the CompTIA Security+ Certification. If you have an extensive Windows investment, the company should have a Microsoft Certified Systems Administrator (MCSA) on staff.

Questions for Your Security Committee

These questions let you examine your current security situation to determine if expanding your security makes sense.

If an incident, such as a tornado or theft, were to strike the operation right now, how long would it take to get back into business?

How long do you have after an occurrence before your customers would begin looking for other vendors?

What would happen to the value of your company if disaster struck?

What would happen if the IT staff wasn't around to restore business systems?

What records are you required by law to maintain? How are you assuring that these records are secure?

What is the potential legal exposure because your organization cannot fulfill contractual obligations?

What would happen if your company's financial records were destroyed? What would that cost?

What incidents have you planned for? When was the plan last reviewed?

A STARTING COMPUTER SECURITY STRATEGY

If you do nothing else do these things:

- Have someone regularly secure the *SANS Top 20* list, reducing your risk by about 80 percent.[157] Step-by-step instructions show how to eliminate each security threat on the list. SANS regularly updates the list with new threats and improved ways to deal with them.
- Implement the password policy recommendations found on page 52.
- Train employees to never open unexpected email attachments. Configure your email server to block email with file attachments used to spread viruses.[158]
- Never run downloaded software unless it has been scanned for viruses and approved by your IT manager.

---

[157] www.sans.org/top20
[158] Such as .bat, .exe, .pif, .scr, and .vbs. These are rarely sent by legitimate users.

- Run your Web server on a separate system unconnected to the rest of your network. If it's compromised, the attacker gets no further.
- Set computer security settings to the highest level and then modify them as needed.
- Many operating systems automatically install services you're not using that open avenues of attack. Ask your IT provider to turn them off and not install them on new computers.

A STARTING PHYSICAL SECURITY STRATEGY

If you do nothing else do these things:

- Shred confidential documents. If you wouldn't want a competitor to see it, shred it.
- Change the locks on your doors and control the keys.
- Increase the light levels outside of your building at night.
- Implement employment agreements with your staff outlining your security policies and expectations.
- Perform background checks on any employee who handles critical assets and data. Start with the employee who is most critical.
- Change employee termination procedures to minimize issues. See more on page 25.

Applications and Success Stories

There are literally thousands of documented security case studies. Most security vendors offer loads of success stories in virtually every industry and application. If you're looking for specific applications in your industry, a quick Internet search will turn up many examples.

This section offers you a few examples of industries where security is part of the business process.

Security in Health Care

No matter where you are in the world, health care providers are under pressure to tighten security. With mandated security requirements and increasing demands for on-line medical records, the business case for security becomes strong.

Encompass Medical Group

The Encompass Medical Group in San Diego, CA has 22 primary care physicians and a full-time support staff of 55.

The Group's foremost concern is information security; HIPAA requires that patient medical records be protected from unauthorized access. Encompass also wanted to use the Internet to exchange information between its 12 offices and laboratory, streamlining operations and unifying accounting, billing, and insurance claim management.

They replaced the slow dialup connections between offices with high-speed Internet connections. With an always-open Internet connection, Encompass needed virus protection and content access control.

At each site, a security appliance from VPN Dynamics[159] running Check Point[160] software intercepts and blocks attacks. Using the Check Point Security Management Portal, IT staff can define and manage security policy from the Internet.

Aside from implementing a strong security policy, Encompass significantly reduced the billing and payment cycle by submitting insurance claims via the Internet to a clearinghouse for large insurers.[161]

TriHealth

TriHealth, Cincinatti, OH provides healthcare coverage to the tri-state area including parts of Indiana, Kentucky, and Ohio. The TriHealth IT department of 85 oversees an infrastructure of more than 100

---

[159] www.vpndynamics.com
[160] www.checkpoint.com
[161] www.checkpoint.com/corporate/success/stories/ encompass.html

applications running on 100 servers and a network that moves voice and data to two hospitals and 120 remote sites.

As part of a two-year plan, TriHealth upgraded its network to provide cheaper, faster, and more secure connectivity to remote sites and doctors' homes; enhance patient privacy; and exceed HIPAA standards. The old network was too slow for new applications and large data files, and didn't offer security that would protect patient privacy. TriHealth chose to replace their proprietary network with Internet access through a Cisco VPN solution.

Using the Cisco SAFE Blueprint, TriHealth's new network security provides the best protection for patients' privacy, observes HIPAA requirements, and cuts network operating costs in half. Physicians have fast, anytime-anywhere access to applications and diagnostic images.[162]

Security in Finance and Banking

Financial services must deliver security because of legislation. Besides, their customers expect protection.

---

[162] www.cisco.com/application/pdf/en/us/guest/
netsol/ns128/c647/ccmigration_09186a0080088a07.pdf

Altamira Investment Services

Altamira Investment Services, Toronto, Ontario, Canada, manages money for mutual funds, pension funds, individuals, corporations, and institutions.

They needed to merge two unconnected networks into a single, secure one offering internal and external email and company data services.

Altamira chose to implement two-factor authentication from RSA[163] so that users could securely access email from the office and home.

Altamira's new network is based on a series of segregated networks serving various user groups and corporate servers with multiple firewalls securing the perimeter and internal networks.

The new network offers high levels of security yet is easy for authorized users to access.[164]

Security in Education

Educators always face the challenge of budget constraints and aging equipment. Many vendors offer special educational discount programs to encourage adoption of their technology.

Pe Ell School

The Pe Ell School is a rural Washington state school serving 311 students with networked computers.

---

[163] www.rsasecurity.com

[164] www.rsasecurity.com/success_stories.asp

A small group of students were exploring Web sites and participating in instant message chats deemed to be inappropriate.

The school selected a SonicWALL content filtering and firewall solution. The technical administrator automatically received daily emailed activity logs identifying blocked activity and the computer that made the attempt.

The school computers are now secure, keeping young prying eyes and fingers out of areas where they shouldn't be.[165]

Grossmont Union High School District

Grossmont Union High School District, El Cajon, CA is an 11-school, 24,000-student district in San Diego County. In 2001, two separate school shootings occurred within two weeks. Despite a US$600,000 budget for police surveillance, students weren't safe.

Grossmont selected Sony's e-Surveillance digital video network system which allows administrators and law enforcement officers to watch and react to emergency situations in real-time. Installation cost was about the same as one salaried police officer for a year.[166]

Just a few months into the system's operation, graffiti, vandalism, and inappropriate use of school

---

[165] www.sonicwall.com/applications/cs_schools.html
[166] www.sony.com/onsite/

facilities had dropped significantly. Cost savings come from a smaller security force, lower cost of school maintenance, and reduced insurance premiums.[167]

Security in Manufacturing

Manufacturing demands efficiencies, high reliability, and a long life cycle for hardware and software.

Harris Corporation

Harris Corporation, Melbourne, FL, produces microwave, broadcast, secure tactical radio, and government communications systems.

Many Harris consultants work on-site at client locations. Both Harris and clients have strict authentication and security policies for network access.

Harris selected Internet-based access through a SSL VPN appliance by SafeNet.[168] A special Web page served up by the appliance is the only publicly accessible point into the network. This mitigates common Web server vulnerabilities because users log on with two-factor authentication before running internal applications. With centralized security control, a user only sees authorized applications.

---

[167] bssc.sel.sony.com/Professional/onsite/pages/news/news_070104_01.htm

[168] www.safenet-inc.com

Employees now securely access critical information from any Web browser from one Web site.[169]

Thomas & Betts

Thomas & Betts, Memphis, TN, is the world's largest manufacturer of power lines, cable, and electrical wiring. Their IT infrastructure consists of more than a dozen high-capacity Web servers plus internal systems.

Most customers order online and pay their invoices electronically, so a stable e-commerce infrastructure is critical. Even a brief shutdown in the order entry system would ripple through their customer base and result in millions of dollars of loss.

Though there were security policies in place, the need for stronger Web server security became apparent when the Code Red worm began to propagate.

Thomas & Betts chose eEye's[170] appliance to secure Web server vulnerabilities between software patches, saving the IT staff more than two months of work a year.[171]

---

[169] www.safenet-inc.com/library/case.asp

[170] www.eeye.com

[171] www.eeye.com/~data/publish/cases/prevention/ ThomasBetts.FILE.pdf

Security in Retail

Retail needs reliable security. If the database systems fail, then inventory shortages show up, affecting the bottom line profitability.

WaWa Food Markets

WaWa Food Markets, Wawa, PA, employs 13,000 people in its corporate headquarters and at more than 550 convenience stores. Their core purpose: "to simplify our customers' daily lives."

Wawa's old dial-up network was taking the "convenience" out of its stores with a 25-second credit card approval time. The company chose to deploy a new network infrastructure to provide faster customer service and to increase business efficiency and security.

Wawa selected a secure Internet-based network solution from Enterasys.[172] The system prioritizes credit card transactions over all other network traffic, dropping approval time to less than five seconds.

Network management tools monitor every piece of equipment at each store. Wireless technology ensures order accuracy and helps managers track goods and inventory. The internal security systems, including fire alarms and security cameras, connect through the network.

---

[172] www.enterasys.com

By eliminating the monthly cost of the dial-up lines, WaWa offset most of the cost of the new network.[173]

Home Depot

Home Depot, Atlanta, GA is the world's largest home improvement retailer with 1,800 stores across North America.

Recently, The Home Depot decided to implement digital video surveillance to ensure a safe and secure environment for employees and customers; to curtail losses from theft, fraud, and error; and to observe behaviors to increase productivity and improve customer service.

They chose Verint[174] video solutions to digitally store, organize, and deliver surveillance camera images. Video can be captured according to rules and behavioral triggers, for example, a cash register opening or a checkout line growing too long.

By connecting to other business systems, the system can instantly video record specific merchandise sales and activities. Loss Prevention Managers at any time can view video for any store under their control.[175]

---

[173] www.enterasys.com/solutions/success/wawa/

[174] www.verint.com

[175] www.verint.com/misc/Case_study_home_depot.pdf

Security in Transportation

Transportation systems have challenging security issues because of multiple locations and continuously changing data.

Interpec Iberica

Interpec Iberica, Madrid, Spain, annually distributes nearly 2 million tons of food products throughout Portugal, Spain, and other European countries.

Interpec has many logistical installations that handle all transactions, from purchasing from foreign producers through delivery to the customer. The network connections transfer data to business systems that manage logistics and purchasing. The old infrastructure had a high monthly cost for telephone lines.

The company selected WatchGuard appliances for firewall and VPN services connecting to the Internet.[176]

Interpec reduced network operating costs by 78 percent, increased security, and sped up information access by 400 percent.[177]

---

[176] www.watchguard.com

[177] www.watchguard.com/docs/casestudies/interpec-iberica_cs.pdf

Republic Services, Inc

Republic Services, Inc., Ft. Lauderdale, FL, provides solid waste collection, disposal and recycling services through 146 collection companies at 300 facilities in 22 states.

Whether it's a staff member from the legal team verifying EPA regulations or supervisors looking for route information, employees must quickly and securely access information, even over slow network connections.

Republic Services selected a Citrix software solution that allows all application processing to occur on central servers.[178] This provides Republic Services with a quick and secure way to deliver information and applications to users in remote offices over any connection.

"When we consider the amount of time we've saved by minimizing help desk costs and eliminating trips to users' desktops, we figure the solution has already paid for itself," said Doug Saunders, Regional IT Director.[179]

---

[178] www.citrix.com

[179] www.citrix.com/site/aboutCitrix/caseStudies/ caseStudy.asp?storyID=3235

Security in Entertainment

Entertainment companies demand efficiency, security, and 100 percent up time because instant gratification is part of their culture.

Downstream

Downstream, Portland, OR, is a media company whose 40 employees create and distribute digital multimedia. They specialize in programs that are downloaded directly to retail outlets, feeding video to more than a hundred stores.

Clients want to review rough cuts of video of over the Internet rather than waiting for mailed tapes or DVDs. Downstream needed a way to deliver and protect media assets, and secure corporate information while employees and partners remotely access the network. Downstream wanted to bring the security management in house for full control over the network rather than relying on an outside provider.

The company selected a Cisco[180] firewall and VPN for secure Internet communications.

Downstream's digital media network now gives the company first-rate video distribution capability. The technical staff has full visibility into the network;

---

[180] www.cisco.com

they can tell when a video server or monitor isn't working in a store.[181]

Padgett Communications

Padgett Communications, Clearwater, FL, measures real-time audience opinions through audience response systems and interactive game show technology. Their network accesses centralized private data.

In a system review, the IT team discovered almost 300 vulnerabilities, and that off-the-shelf firewall and antivirus software wasn't enough to secure the network.

Founder, Todd Padgett concluded that a third-party managed security service provider (MSSP) could best do the job. Handing off security activities to expert security engineers freed his staff to focus on the core business.

They went from 298 vulnerabilities to 24 (1 high, 4 medium, 1 low, 18 information) in a matter of days using outsourcing and eEye vulnerability assessment tools.[182]

---

[181] http://www.cisco.com/application/pdf/en/us/guest/netsol/ns423/c647/cdccont_0900aecd800f597c.pdf

[182] www.eeye.com/html/resources/cases/assessment/index.html

Security in Communications

Communications companies demand stability, security, long equipment life, and maximum value for the cost.

Interland

Interland, Atlanta, GA, is a Web hosting service company for small and medium-sized businesses.

Interland's approach to security became too expensive for their clients. They needed to create a security infrastructure that met client cost and performance needs.

Interland selected Juniper Networks NetScreen® firewall and IPSec VPN solution because of the throughput required for Web hosting.[183]

Now Interland has expanded service offerings and is seeing increased revenue growth while offering more secure access to corporate data.[184]

Security in Government

Governments aren't as influenced by market pressure when it comes to purchases when compared with other companies. They aren't forced to be efficient or competitive. Yet most governments try to do their best with what they have.

---

[183] www.juniper.net

[184] www.juniper.net/solutions/customer_profiles/

City of Anaheim

The City of Anaheim, CA, serves 340,000 residents over about 50 square miles. Two thousand employees, including public safety services, use 2,400 networked PCs.

Key challenges: virus infections from compromised laptop computers of employees and vendors, keeping out unauthorized network users, and new applications demanding more network capacity.

The City chose to build a secure network infrastructure with an Enterasys secure network.[185]

A policy-based network limits guest access while ensuring authentication for all internal users; improving security and reducing IT management costs from configuration changes. Dynamic intrusion response detects and isolates viruses. The network's increased throughput supports next-generation applications to move the City to a paperless environment.

The new system uses almost half the number of IT staff to maintain when compared with other network systems. Longer service life of new equipment frees up funds for crucial services like fire and police.[186]

---

[185] www.enterasys.com

[186] www.enterasys.com/solutions/success/anaheim.pdf

APPENDIX A -
USEFUL WEB SITES

These sites are a good starting point for security resources. A quick Internet search will give you many more options.

Definitions

If you see a computer or security technology word that you don't know, go to www.whatis.com and you'll get the answer. You can also access tutorial information at this site when you want to dig deeper.

Hoax Reference Sites

A quick check at these reference sites will uncover most hoax email you receive.

- CIAC (Computer Incident Advisory Capability, Department of Energy) Hoax site: http://hoaxbusters.ciac.org
- Symantec Hoax site: securityresponse.symantec.com/ avcenter/hoax.html

- TrendMicro Hoax site:
  www.trendmicro.com/vinfo/
  hoaxes/hoax.asp
- You can submit suspicious email to
  hoaxes@trendmicro.com for analysis.
- Urban Legends Reference:
  www.snopes.com

Information Systems Security

Information Technology Solution Providers Alliance

www.itspa.net – The ITSPA is a national non-profit alliance of solution providers who help small and mid-sized businesses purchase, customize, and install technology equipment and software.

TechTarget.com Learning Zone

TechTarget.com – On-line training specializing in IT management and strategy, e-commerce, operating system security, and more.

The Security-Specific Search Engine

SearchSecurity.com – Offers a variety of newsletters or Web casts dedicated to security. The site offers security-specific daily news, more than 1,000 links, and interaction with leading industry experts.

Security and Privacy Research Center

www.cio.com/research/security – From creating and implementing a security policy to dealing with rogue programmers, the CIO Security and Privacy Research Center can help with ideas to keep your network and site secure.

Computerworld Knowledge Center

www.computerworld.com/securitytopics/security – Leading with the latest security headlines, Computerworld's site includes upcoming events, links to vendors, security statistics and reviews, as well as online discussions.

Electronic Privacy Information Center

www.epic.org – This site from the Electronic Privacy Information Center (EPIC), a public interest research center, covers the gamut of online privacy issues.

Computer Security Institute

www.gocsi.com – Publishes the annual FBI/CSI computer crime and security survey. Educates computer and network security professionals about protecting information assets.

The CERT Coordination Center

www.cert.org – Web site for the CERT Coordination Center at Carnegie Mellon University, a major reporting center for Internet and network security vulner-abilities.

Information Systems Security Association

www.issa.org – A non-profit association for informa-tion security professionals that facilitates interaction and education to promote secure information systems management practices.

Center for Internet Security

www.cisecurity.org – CIS members identify security threats of greatest concern and develop practical methods to reduce the threats. Provides methods and tools to improve, measure, monitor, and compare the security status of your Internet-connected systems and appliances. CIS is not tied to any specific product or service.

NIST's Computer Security Resource Center

csrc.nist.gov – Resources from the National Institute of Standards and Technology's Computer Security Division.

Physical Security

ASIS International

www.asisonline.org – Formerly the American Society for Industrial Security, this is the preeminent interna-tional organization for security professionals.

Canadian Security Association

www.canasa.org – CANASA represents the intrusion alarm industry in Canada.

National Security Institute

nsi.org – The site features industry and product news, computer alerts, travel advisories, a calendar of events, a directory of products and services, and an on-line security library.

Security Industry Association

www.siaonline.org – The trade association of security product manufacturers and service providers.

Check Guarantee Companies

Contact these companies to report ID theft concerning checks or to use their services to prevent accepting fraudulent checks.

- SCAN: www.scanassist. com (800) 262-7771
- National Check Fraud Service: www.ckfraud.org (843) 571-2143
- TeleCheck: www.telecheck.com (800) 366-2425
- CrossCheck: www.cross-check.com (800) 552-1900
- Equifax Check Systems: (800) 437-5120
- International Check Services: (800) 526-5380

APPENDIX B -
BIBLIOGRAPHY

Avoiding Disaster: How to Keep Your Business Going When Catastrophe Strikes, John Laye, Wiley, 2002

Building an Information Security Awareness Program, Mark B. Desman, Auerbach Publishing, 2001

Computer Security Basics, Debby Russell, Sr. G.T Gangemi, O'Reilly, 1991

Contemporary Security Management, John L. Fay, Butterworth-Heinemann, 2001

Contingency Planning and Disaster Recovery: A Small Business Guide, Donna R. Childs, Stefan Dietrich. Wiley, 2002

Design and Evaluation of Physical Protection Systems, The, Mary Lynn Garcia, Butterworth Heinemann, 2001

Disaster Recovery Handbook, The: A Step-by-Step Plan to Ensure Business Continuity and Protect Vital Operations, Facilities, and Assets, Michael Wallace, Lawrence Webber, AMACOM, 2004

Disaster Recovery Planning: Strategies for Protecting Critical Information Assets, Jon William Toigo, Prentice Hall, 2002

Effective Physical Security (3rd edition), Lawrence J. Fennelly, Butterworth Heinemann, 2003

Effective Security Management, (4ᵗʰ Edition), Charles A. Sennewald, Butterworth-Heinemann, 2003

Encyclopedia of Security Management: Techniques and Technology, John L. Fay, Butterworth-Heinemann, 1993

Introduction to Security (7ᵗʰ edition), Robert J. Fischer, Butterworth-Heinemann, 2003

Manager's Handbook for Corporate Security, The: Establishing and Managing a Successful Assets Protection Program, Gerald L. Kovacich, Edward P. Halibozek, Butterworth-Heinemann, 2002

Risk Analysis and the Security Survey, James F. Broder, Butterworth-Heinemann, 1999

Security Planning and Disaster Recovery, Eric Maiwald, William Sieglein, McGraw-Hill Osborne Media, 2002

Wireless Security, Merritt Maxim, David Pollino, McGraw-Hill, 2002

Writing Information Security Policies, Scott Barman, Sams, 2001

ABOUT THE AUTHOR

Mark S.A. Smith is an electrical engineer, computer programmer, hardware salesman, software marketer, and author. Mark focuses on how to rapidly create sound business decisions in a fast-paced business world. He delivers innovative business strategies for entrepreneurial thinkers, executives, and sales professionals. Mark's an expert in creating instantly implementable tactics to achieve real business success.

Mark authored the critically-acclaimed *Linux in the Boardroom: How Linux is Changing Corporate Computing and What Executives Need to Know and Do About It*. He co-authored business best-sellers *Guerrilla Trade Show Selling*, *Guerrilla TeleSelling*, and *Guerrilla Negotiating*.

Recognized by his peers, Mark is a full member of the Society for the Advancement of Consulting. Membership requires stringent proof of performance, expertise, and excellence in consulting. A veteran professional speaker, he is past president of the National Speakers Association, Colorado chapter. Mark regularly appears at top industry events as a speaker, panel moderator, or emcee.

He co-created the wildly successful Executive Assessment business case creation tool for IBM, writing approximately 70 product-specific versions for IBM's major software brands, including DB2,® WebSphere,® Lotus,® Tivoli,® and Start Now.™

Today he's president of Outsource Channel Executives, Inc, an organization that helps companies build new sales channels and get more out the channels they have. By uniquely combining product knowledge with sales and marketing skills, the company creates programs that instill excitement and confidence in people who have to sell.

Mark is available for consulting and speaking engagements. Contact him through www.OCEinc.com.

INDEX